# THE MAN COMES AROUND

## THE SPIRITUAL JOURNEY OF

# JOHNNY CASH

DAVE URBANSKI

FOREWORD BY JARS OF CLAY'S DAN HASELTINE

Published by Relevant Books
A division of Relevant Media Group, Inc.

www.relevantbooks.com
www.relevantmediagroup.com



Design: Relevant Solutions
www.relevant-solutions.com
Matthew Crow, Aaron Martin



For information:
RELEVANT MEDIA GROUP, INC.
POST OFFICE BOX 951127
LAKE MARY, FL 32795
407-333-7152

Library of Congress Control Number: 2003096211
International Standard Book Number: 0-9729276-7-0

03 04 05 06 9 8 7 6 5 4 3 2 1

Printed in the United States of America

TO MY BRIDE, JENNY—

MY GREATEST JOY ON EARTH.

# ACKNOWLEDGMENTS

This book would have been infinitely difficult to complete had it not been for the efforts and encouragement of my wife, Jenny Anticoli, a gifted writer who (in addition to her selfless transcribing on my behalf) offered invaluable criticism at a critical juncture during the early stages of my writing. Her words and insight inspired me for the duration of the project. I love you, Sweetie.

My wonderful family, a vast and far-reaching clan, requires alphabetical thanks. So a big shout out to: the Anticolis, the Kenneys, the Stricks, the Tobins, the Urbanskis—and all those whom they love.

Several individuals contributed generously and tirelessly to my research efforts (as well as to my mental and spiritual health): Rich Campbell, Richard "Paw" Strick, Ralph Bingham, John Buckley, Lou Carlozo, Kathleen Aisling, Jeff and Sharon Bjorck, and John Raymond and Lisa Waydin at Zondervan—you're all gems.

My fellow laborers at Youth Specialties were quite accommodating as my schedule (not to mention my desk and office) grew even more cluttered than usual. Mark Oestreicher, Rick Marschall, and Jay Howver—all experienced writers—offered invaluable advice along the way. Thanks guys.

To Cameron and Cara and the rest of the Relevant crew—thanks for the shot.

I also wish to express my appreciation for my mother and father, Margaret Tobin Strick and Victor R. Urbanski. They never failed to encourage my writing through the years, and whether they know it or not, I took much from their uncommon abilities to communicate in written form. I'm forever grateful, Mom and Dad.

Last but quite opposite of least: Thank you, Jesus, for carrying me through—and for dreams come true.

FOREWORD

# THE SAINT IN BLACK

**BY DAN HASELTINE**
**LEAD SINGER, JARS OF CLAY**

I grew up in Massachusetts in a time classic rock seemed to rule the airwaves. But in the late '70s and early '80s when other kids were filling their veins with Led Zeppelin and Deep Purple, my father would carry me to bluegrass festivals. My first concert experience was a triple bill: Alabama, Statler Brothers, and Juice Newton in Hartford, Connecticut. And for the amount of exposure I had to this type of music, I was proud to say I built up quite a resistance.

I was never a real fan of country music. My short life had nothing in common with the things people talked about in those songs. I loved rock 'n' roll. I spent hours hiding out listening to the thunder of Van Halen, Rush, The Who, and Queen. But if I happened to be riding in my father's

Volkswagen bug, that radio was locked onto WIXY Country 16. (The only thing more abrasive than the ping of the diesel engine that always brought on a bout of carsickness was the metallic ring of the screaming little speakers.) It was an AM station controlled by disc jockeys with a genuine love for the music of country legends: George Jones, Tammy Wynette, Emmylou Harris, Loretta Lynn, Willie Nelson, and of course, Johnny Cash. My earliest memories of family outings were to the movies. With the exception of the time I was privy to a double feature of *Creepshow* and *Twilight Zone the Movie*, the films we watched were about the country music life, movies like *Honeysuckle Rose* and *The Coal Miner's Daughter*.

It was not until my mid-twenties that I started seeing other forms of music, pop—in particular—and rock music, lose their ability to dig deep and express things that were not so temporal. Country and bluegrass music had stood the test of time. Though I was not much a fan of these in my youth, I have grown to love the honesty and the realism that they hold as one of their foundational characteristics.

Throughout my life, few singers stayed firmly planted in my periphery the way Johnny Cash did. But as a kid I knew so little about the Man in Black that the image I gathered from the songs "Wanted Man," "Starkville City Jail," and "San Quentin," made me think this Johnny Cash fellow must have killed a few men and be serving a sentence at Folsom Prison where the legendary recordings took place.

There is a language that exposed men use. And a posture that only men living behind brick and barbed wire exhibit in the exercise of chipping away at guilt and regret with the tool of time. They speak in expressions that mix together the shame of being caught with the strange freedom of being found out.

Cash carried himself with a similar stance that gave the prisoners he performed for at Folsom Prison, San Quentin, and others a sense that he understood their story. Even though he was not a prisoner in the judicial sense of the word, he was well aquainted with addictions that stripped away true freedom. And so he spoke with authority and credibility to those serving time for the mistakes they had made along the way.

Now, twenty years after being introduced to the legendary songwriter, I still find him to be one of the most fascinating musical icons of the last fifty years.

Johnny Cash has always given voice to men who believe that God is real and life is hard, that sin is real but so is redemption. And when a man like this sings "Amazing Grace," he sings it with the authority of one who needs every drop of blood spilled to gain the benefit of such a necessary pardon. And by ways only God can tell, he had reconciled with his weaknesses and lived a life of transparency that gave voice to both his struggles and his devotion to God.

A life lived without pretense and hiding seems foreign to most of us. We often mistake it for an abuse of grace. But to those who have felt the gut level need for grace and been embraced by mercy, it is an expression of relief. We do not need to hide anymore. We do not need to lie anymore. We need to live and can live with our weaknesses and rough edges exposed.

The Gospel has always found its greatest ally in the likes of those who wander the earth exposed to its quiet beauty as well as its violent tantrums. Perhaps Cash was acutely aware of this when he gravitated toward the stories of cowboys and gunslingers. There is something wildly reverant about the men who worked the unsettled West world that spread out under the big blue sky, just like the men Jesus gravitated to: fishermen, farmers, and all the kinds of people who knew their greatest battles were not against the people around them, but rather against things much less controllable, things like the wind, sun, tide, and thunder. The ultra-human songs about the wornout and brokenhearted, the struck down but not destroyed seem to have a similar foundation and a consistent declaration that the world is frustrated and the people in it are weak and foolish. And so we must lay ourselves bare to the only thing that can save us: grace.

I turned on the radio one day after the journey of Johnny Cash found its way to the gates of glory. It was a continual playlist of Cash's music. Radio stations that never played a Johnny Cash song were paying tribute to a musical legend, an honest sojourner, and a rough and rugged common man, who began his career with the hopes of singing gospel songs and found himself in the company of convicts and cowboys, presidents and preachers, and ultimately sharing by example a godly perspective that there was little difference in the content of the great hymns of old and the stories of life as a wanted man with a price to pay.

The greatest of all storylines, the one that makes movies, songs, poems, and novels move us at our core, is the story of redemption. It is the story of taking broken down things and making them new again. As you read the chapters of this book, you will find a thread of redemption in the life of this man, the kind of redemption that makes a man want to tell his story to everyone he can. To paraphrase Ernest Hemingway: The world breaks or kills us all, and the ones who survive will be stronger in the broken places. From the beginning of Cash's life in the fields of Dyess Colony to the rooms of Sun Studios and the drug filled, sleepless nights in the back of a '53 Cadillac, and onto the roads of Hendersonville, Tennessee, there are reasons to rejoice that God found His way into the broken places of Johnny Cash and filled them with faith. Cash came away stronger, wiser, and taller.

I believe the saints have welcomed home one of their own. And if it is true that the journey we take toward redemption is the continual climax to the Gospel-driven life, let us reflect on the life of one of the saints, one of the sinners, one of the artists, one of the icons of our time and culture.

His name is Johnny Cash, and this is his journey.

# CONTENTS

# A ONE-MAN MT. RUSHMORE OF AMERICAN ROCK

IT HAPPENED ON THE NIGHT OF August 28, 2003.

The annoyingly hip—and often just plain annoying—Video Music Awards were taking place, as they do at the close of every summer, in New York City. The youth-culture savvy tastemakers at MTV readied moonmen for the sexiest, coolest, and baddest in the biz. And they all strutted their stuff down the red carpet and into the deafening confines of Radio City Music Hall.

But while Madonna was busy kissing Britney and Eminem was busy beating the boogers out of a Crank Yanker puppet, one inescapable fact floated around the proceedings like a giant phantom—the crowd knew it; the artists knew it. But nary a soul was talking. It was a palpable truth that even most veejays couldn't approach or categorize or explain away.

A maverick nominee was up for six awards that night. An outsider. A musician who never much cared for the trappings of pop culture, and cared even less about the trappings of the music establishment. One mean-eyed cat who'd just as soon put the likes of 50 Cent and Fred Durst over his knee.

His age (seventy-one) and craggy, beautifully broken visage (as seen in his nominated video, "Hurt") in the company of well-oiled, pretty vacant bods vying for the next nanosecond of attention was akin to a DaVinci sharing shelf space with a paint-by-numbers job. Just didn't fit. Different universes.

But despite reports that Johnny Cash would indeed make an appearance at the VMAs, doctors decided the day before that his stomach ailment made travel impossible, so he opted to watch the proceedings from his hospital room in Nashville.

Kurt Loder, the venerable elder statesman of MTV, traveled to Cash's home in Hendersonville, Tennessee, for an interview just before the awards shindig. Upon Loder's return, he posted this note on MTV.com: "Johnny Cash is a one-man Mt. Rushmore of American rock/folk/country/whatever. He's 71 years old now, and his video for 'Hurt'—an emotional train wreck of a clip unlike anything else I believe I've ever seen—is up for six—six!—Video Music Awards next week. I hope he wins 'em all."

It's for the best that Cash couldn't make the trip—paint-by-numbers won big that night in Manhattan, leaving DaVinci alone on that higher plane he'll forever occupy.

In the midst of the glitz, glamour, chest-thumping, and backslapping, however, was one memorable moment of acknowledgment, of clarity, of sanity—and it came from an unlikely source: Justin Timberlake. Indefinitely on hiatus from *NSync, the heartthrob Michael Jackson wannabe took home awards in three highly touted VMA categories, including Best Male Video. It was a category Cash was also nominated for.

Approaching the podium with decidedly less bravado and white-boy street cred (that still fools nobody), Timberlake wisely suggested a recount was in order.

"My grandfather raised me on Johnny Cash," he said without a hint of irony. "I'm from Tennessee. And I think he deserves this more than any of us in here tonight. So, I guess in some cool way, I share this award with him. And he deserves a round of applause." Well said.

A fair amount of posts to MTV.com, however, weren't as kind to the network in regard to Cash's near shutout ("Hurt" did nab a moonman for Best Cinematography, a minor accolade):

- Joeinsactown noted that "Hurt" is "one of the greatest videos I have ever seen. The first time I saw it I just sat there stunned. It was his life story. I've never watched a video more intently. I guess it didn't have enough exploitation of women to get a MTV award."
- Ohiomyfriend proclaimed "this was MTV's lowest point in its 20-year history."

In short, the Man in Black strikes again.

## A CLUSTER OF ENIGMAS

Johnny Cash's musical accomplishments are storied and staggering. He occupies spots in the Rock and Roll Hall of Fame, the Songwriter's Hall of Fame, and the Country Music Hall of Fame—he, in fact, was the first living person ever inducted into the latter. He sold 50 million albums, recorded more than 1,500 songs, boasted fourteen number-one hits, won scads of awards—including eleven Grammys—and is mentioned in the same breath as The Beatles when it comes to musical impact. (Indeed, Cash even outsold The Beatles—and everybody else—in 1969, ringing up 6.5 million albums at the registers.)

His legendary bass-baritone was a force of nature. Equal parts rolling thunder and John the Baptist, when Cash sang or spoke, his voice commanded attention. And respect. And believability. More than most preachers who've ever stood in a pulpit, Johnny Cash's was the voice of truth. One writer described the Cash delivery as "deep as an open wound. It broods, it glowers, it chills."[1]

Another declared Cash's voice as "earthy-deep, ominous sometimes, resonant, virile, untrained, unconventional. It can be lonely and haunting, coming out as practically a dirge, and the next minute be booming happily on a jumping rock piece. Cash has a blue tonality, does not sustain his notes, does not sing by the scale or sing sharps, and he slides into his flats. 'He is constantly bending the tone,' an academic observer says. 'He is singing what's inside of him, searching in a haunting way for a note that isn't there. He decorates his melody according to his own interpretation.'"[2]

But more importantly, throughout his magical career that ended just shy of the half-century mark when he died from diabetes complications on September 12, 2003—just two weeks after the 2003 VMAs—Cash tore apart the rulebook more than once, paving the way for other artists to do the same; he built countless bridges across once-unassailable chasms that separated musicians and musical genres; he played concerts that 99 percent of other artists would never consider (Folsom, San Quentin); he always stood up for the underdog (the poor, Native Americans, prisoners, and others) and always stood up to the oppressive (the Ku Klux Klan, whom Cash once threatened with forty lashes from a snake whip); and he beat just about every odd that was stacked against him.

And it's for those reasons that pinning down Johnny Cash in any way, shape, or form is impossible. He made it impossible. He never intended to be categorized or pigeonholed. He recorded with Bob Dylan, then turned around and played for Richard Nixon. He embraced the radical social justice movements of the '60s and flew high Old Glory. He protested Vietnam and played for the troops. And please, don't limit him as a "country" music artist, either—he hated that: "I don't see trying to put something in a bag and keep it there," Cash said of those who try to define his style and intent. "My music—I just call it Johnny Cash-type music. I don't imitate anybody."[3]

"I always kind of knew exactly where I fit ... in this music business," Cash once said. "I never felt any competition from anybody else. I always did my thing ... the way I felt it, the way I saw it, the way it feels right to me."[4]

The revelation is that Cash lived long enough and hard enough to embody a host of personas—and they're all true. Songwriter. Six-string strummer. Storyteller. Country boy. Rock star. Folk hero. Preacher. Poet. Drug addict. Rebel. Sinner. Saint. Victim. Survivor. Home wrecker. Husband. Father. Klan target. Outlaw. Moviemaker. Jailbird. Jailhouse troubadour. Truth teller. Novelist. Salesman. War protestor. Patriot. Hell raiser. Heavenly guide. And many more—you name 'em.

As songwriting friend Kris Kristofferson recently said, "He's as comfortable with the poor and prisoners as he is with presidents. He's crossed over all age boundaries. I like to think of him as Abraham Lincoln with a wild side."[5]

Cash's cluster of enigmas was so impenetrably deep that even those closest to him never got to see every part of him, every thought, every emotion.

"I think Johnny's as complex as anything God or man put on this earth," his brother Tommy once noted. "He's a man of uncommon characteristics, mentally or physically. Even though you're his brother, or his wife, or his mother, you never know him completely. I've felt myself at times trembling because of my inadequacy around him."[6]

Cash's spiritual core was no exception.

A writer once tried to paint Cash into a corner, baiting him to acknowledge a single denominational persuasion at the center of his heart. Finally, Cash laid down the law: "I—as a believer that Jesus of Nazareth, a Jew, the Christ of the Greeks, was the Anointed One of God (born of the seed of David, upon faith as Abraham has faith, and it was accounted to him for righteousness)—am grafted onto the true vine, and am one of the heirs of God's covenant with Israel."

"What?" the writer replied.

"I'm a Christian," Cash shot back. "Don't put me in another box."[7]

Despite his Baptist/Pentecostal upbringing, Cash was never terribly concerned about denominations. Or about nickel-and-dime theology. Or about tedious doctrinal parsing. "In my travels to Europe, Asia, and Australia, many times I have remembered and realized more fully that the Gospel is the only doctrine that really works, and it works for all men," he once declared. "But when this or that denomination begins to feel, or still worse, begins to teach that their particular interpretation of the Word opens the only door to heaven, then I feel it's dangerous."[8]

So, exactly what "kind" of Christian was Cash?

A staunch, conservative, Bible thumper? It sure seems so if you read the introduction to his 1986 novel about the life of the apostle Paul, *Man in White*: "Please understand that I believe the Bible, the whole Bible, to be the infallible, indisputable Word of God. I have been careful to take no liberties with the timeless Word."[9]

But based on a passage from his 1997 autobiography, Cash doesn't seem as steadfast: "Once I learned what the Bible is—the inspired Word of God (most of it anyway) … "[10] (To be fair, he continues this shadow of doubt with a gushing endorsement of Scripture, noting how "truly exciting" it is to discover new interpretations and applications to his own life.)

Further, it certainly can be argued that Cash was a private man and preferred to keep his faith to himself. Stu Carnall, an early tour manager recalled, "Johnny's an individualist, and he's a loner. He's also unpredictable … He's a talker, and he can talk plenty about anything—but not about religion. We'd be on the road for weeks at a time, staying at motels and hotels along the way. While the other members of the troupe would sleep in, Johnny would disappear for a few hours. When he returned, if anyone asked where he'd been, he'd answer straight faced, 'to church.'"[11]

"I don't compromise my religion," Cash once declared. "If I'm with someone who doesn't want to talk about it, I don't talk about it. I don't impose myself on anybody in any way, including religion. When you're imposing you're offending, I feel. Although I am evangelical, and I'll give the message to anyone that wants to hear it, or anybody that is willing to listen. But if they let me know that they don't want to hear it, they ain't never going to hear it from me. If I think they don't want to hear it, then I will not bring it up."[12]

In short, "telling others is part of our faith all right, but the way we live it speaks louder than we can say it," Cash said. "The gospel of Christ must always be an open door with a welcome sign for all."[13]

But put Cash in front of a microphone … and, as you might have guessed, anything could happen.

"I'm not here tonight to exalt Johnny Cash … " he told an audience during a show following his dramatic rededication to Christ in the early '70s. "I'm standing here as an entertainer, as a performer, as a singer who is supporting the Gospel of Jesus Christ. I'm here to invite you to listen to the good news that will be laid out for you, to analyze it, and see if you don't think it's the best way to live."[14]

Cash also made major headlines when he shared his faith on *The Johnny Cash Show*, a popular variety program on ABC that ran from 1969 to 1971: "Well, folks," he began, "I've introduced lots of hymns and gospel songs on this show. I just want to make it clear that I'm feeling what I'm singing about in this next one. I am a Christian ... I want to dedicate this song to the proposition that God is the victor in my life. I'd be nothing without Him. I want to get in a good lick right now for Number One."[15]

(Yet there are those in the Church who questioned his decision, during one momentous episode of the show, to sing the controversial lyric, "wishing Lord that I was stoned" from Kris Kristofferson's hit "Sunday Morning Coming Down.")

And while Cash longed to play only gospel music from the start—and would have if Sam Phillips hadn't nixed his desires as economically unfeasible for Sun Records—he never shied away from performing secular-themed songs in the studio or on the concert stage throughout his career.

A huge influence on Cash in this potentially problematic area was, believe it or not, evangelist Billy Graham, who sought out Johnny in the early '70s when he heard of his commitment to God.

"He and I spent a lot of time talking the issues over, and we determined that I wasn't called to be an evangelist ... " Cash recalled of his first face-to-face conversations with Graham. "He had advised me to keep singing 'Folsom Prison Blues' and 'A Boy Named Sue' and all those other outlaw songs if that's what people wanted to hear and then, when it came time to do a gospel song, give it everything I had. Put my heart and soul into all my music, in fact; never compromise; take no prisoners. 'Don't apologize for who you are and what you've done in the past,' he told me. 'Be who you are and do what you do.'"[16]

"I think I just like to share my faith, you know?" he said in later years. "I don't preach to people. I don't ever push it on anybody, and I wouldn't sing a gospel song on any show if I didn't think the people would enjoy it. They seem to enjoy those as much or more than anything else. It's not that I'm proselytizing. I'm not out there tryin' to convince people, just to spread a little good news."[17]

As it turns out, Cash quickly became a welcome figure at both Billy Graham Crusades and on the ostentatious stages of Las Vegas. And while he insisted that these (seemingly) diametrically opposed venues were equally home in his heart and mind, U2's Bono wasn't convinced: "Johnny Cash doesn't sing to the damned, he sings with the damned, and sometimes you feel he might prefer their company … "[18]

## A WALKING CONTRADICTION

Cash's daughter, singer-songwriter Rosanne Cash, once pointed out that "my father was raised a Baptist, but he has the soul of a mystic. He's a profoundly spiritual man, but he readily admits to a continual attraction for all seven deadly sins."[19]

"There's nothing hypocritical about it," Cash told *Rolling Stone* scribe Anthony DeCurtis. "There is a spiritual side to me that goes real deep, but I confess right up front that I'm the biggest sinner of them all." To Cash, even his near deadly bout with drug addiction contained a crucial spiritual element. "I used drugs to escape, and they worked pretty well when I was younger. But they devastated me physically and emotionally—and spiritually … [they put me] in such a low state that I couldn't communicate with God. There's no lonelier place to be. I was separated from God, and I wasn't even trying to call on Him. I knew that there was no line of communication. But He came back. And I came back."[20]

Years after his return to the land of the living, Cash once got a visit from U2 members Bono and Adam Clayton who were driving across the U.S., taking in the local colors. The three of them sat around a table before their meal, and Cash floored the two Irishmen with an incredible prayer of thanksgiving to God. Then, without skipping a beat, he raised his head and quipped, "Sure miss the drugs, though."[21]

Cash sums up his soul's murky landscape—if that's possible—better than anybody else: "I'm still a Christian, as I have been all my life. Beyond that I get complicated. I endorse Kris Kristofferson's line about me: 'He's a walking contradiction, partly truth and partly fiction.' I also like Rosanne's line: 'He believes what he says, but that don't make him a saint.' I do believe what I say. There are levels of honesty, though."[22]

Sigh.

At this juncture, you may be asking why the book you're holding is attempting to figure out the spiritual nature of this man—a puzzling personality who once implored, "Please don't tell anybody how I feel about anything … unless I told you in the last few days."[23]

The answer? It's attempting nothing of the sort. The sole purpose of this book is to focus on the wild, incredible ups and downs of Cash's spiritual journey. It's a chronicle of his highs and lows, a record of the ebb and flow of his soul's story.

And like many such journeys, Cash's was a roller coaster experience—though his twists and turns and plunges have been more intense than the average person's ... and, well, there were a lot more of them.

Cash began life close to church, close to the earth, and close to gospel music, but his earliest singles for Sun Records hit the secular path rather than the gospel road he hoped Sam Phillips would let him follow; Phillips' preference for the former led to big hits from Cash right from the start, and he immediately became a slave to the road, soon making millions of dollars and winning over millions of fans; he battled through a lot of death through the years—including his big brother Jack's, his parents', his longtime guitarist Luther Perkins', and especially his wife of thirty-five years, June Carter Cash's—but Cash somehow eluded the Grim Reaper's snares despite feeding his frame with truckloads of uppers and downers over the better part of the 1960s; he enjoyed a creative and spiritual renaissance in the late '60s and early '70s, a run that not only sealed his status as the father of American music but proved a blueprint for what would soon become contemporary Christian music; and then, just when it appeared his career was sputtering to a halt in the late '80s and early '90s, Cash confounded everyone by becoming the "it" artist once again, boldly interpreting eclectic song mixtures that mined alternative rock and bygone standards.

And while his body suffered under the strain wrought by years of abuse, Cash's mind stayed strong ... and his spirit stayed stronger.

"Being a Christian isn't for sissies," Cash said once. "It takes a real man to live for God—a lot more man than to live for the devil, you know? If you really want to live right these days, you gotta be tough."[24]

What's more, he's intimately aware of the hard truths about living God's way: "If you're going to be a Christian, you're going to change. You're going to lose some old friends, not because you want to, but because you need to."[25]

## "I DON'T GIVE UP"

Especially since June's death in May 2003, many wondered how much longer Cash could hang on to life—it's not uncommon, after all, for longtime spouses to die in close succession to each other. And that's exactly what happened.

But you have to admit those were fightin' words to Cash. In fact, shortly after June's death, Cash headed back into the studio to begin work on more songs with fellow rebel and producer of nearly a decade, Rick Rubin. (Truth be told, Cash's last two albums, *American III: Solitary Man* and *American IV: The Man Comes Around*, were both reckoned as his farewell offerings.)

"He kind of made a decision," Rubin told *Billboard*. "He called me a couple of days after June passed and said that he really has dedicated his life to work and wants to be busy all the time and focused on songs. That's what he wants to do, so that's what we're going to do [and] that's what we've been doing."[26]

And in his final days, despite moment-by-moment battles with diabetes, glaucoma (which cost him well over half of his vision), asthma, and a progressive, debilitating case of autonomic neuropathy (which deadened his nerve endings, complicated his other ailments, and pretty much confined Cash to a wheelchair during his waking hours), the Man in Black was anything but in a black mood. In fact, he was celebrating life—sopping up every second he could, while he could.

"I'm thrilled to death with life," he told Larry King during a recent interview. "Life is—the way God has given it to me—was just a platter. A golden platter of life laid out there for me. It's been beautiful."

Observers were continually amazed with the grace Cash exuded despite the legion of forces working against him. "He looks more frail than imposing, propped up in his black leather recliner," one writer noted. "Yet … it's remarkable just how vital, even unassailable, Cash and his craggy baritone remain … and while Cash's stentorian vocals may sound tattered, they still convey an almost biblical authority, a reverberant mix of judgment, hope, and, above all, steadfastness."[27]

"I don't give up," he told Larry King. "I don't give up … and it's not out of frustration and desperation that I say 'I don't give up.' I don't give up because I don't give up. I don't believe in it."

Amen to that.

# I AM BOUND FOR THE PROMISED LAND

THE 1930S HAD NOT BEEN KIND to the once-mighty American farmer. Ravaged by the Great Depression, those charged with growing food and raw materials for the rest of the country (and the rest of the world) were just as down and out as the next guy. Prices plunged, money disappeared, and countless acres were dying.

But when President Franklin Delano Roosevelt stepped in with his New Deal, Ray Cash was all ears.

What interested the World War I veteran and struggling family man most was Roosevelt's Federal Emergency Relief Administration. Under its auspices, folks were relocated to government-purchased land they could pay back over time with crop proceeds. And if selected, they'd receive a barn and a mule to work the twenty-acre plots.

Certainly sounded like a deal—especially in the face of all the obstacles facing the elder Cash.

"My father rode the rails looking for work of any kind, anywhere to make a few dollars to feed us on," Johnny Cash wrote in the liner notes of his Grammy-winning 1996 album, *Unchained.*

"We lived by [the] railroad track that I rode with my uncle on at the age of three. When my father had exhausted every effort to find work near home, he'd hop a freight going anywhere if the doors were empty on the boxcars. He'd come back the same way, days or weeks later, jumping off in front of our house, as the train slowed down to stop in Kingsland." The sound of the Rock Island locomotive whistle across the cotton fields might mean Cash's father was coming home with a few dollars—or maybe nothing at all.[1]

So in the winter of 1935, Ray and Carrie Rivers Cash and their six youngins (including three-year-old J.R.—Johnny's given name until 1950 when Air Force brass asked him to choose a proper moniker for better record-keeping) piled into an old flatbed truck and made their way from their windowless shack that hugged the edge of those railroad tracks in Kingsland, Arkansas, to the new Dyess Colony Scheme, 14,000 fertile, swampy acres in the northeast corner of the state, just down the road a piece from the Mississippi River.

It was on that freezing, bumpy ride to Dyess that Johnny Cash was introduced to gospel music. The tune was "I Am Bound for the Promised Land," and it couldn't have been more appropriate for their journey—and their destination. The lyrics of the old spiritual filled the Cash family with a hope they hadn't experienced in quite a while:

*On Jordan's stormy banks I stand,*
*And cast a wishful eye*
*To Canaan's fair and happy land,*
*Where my possessions lie*

*I am bound for the promised land,*
*I am bound for the promised land;*
*Oh who will come and go with me?*
*I am bound for the promised land*

For the dirt-poor Cash clan, there would be no more wandering to make ends meet or to keep food on the table.

*O the transporting, rapturous scene,*
*That rises to my sight!*
*Sweet fields arrayed in living green,*
*And rivers of delight!*

*There generous fruits that never fail,*
*On trees immortal grow;*
*There rocks and hills, and brooks and vales,*
*With milk and honey flow*

*O'er all those wide extended plains*
*Shines one eternal day;*
*There God the Son forever reigns,*
*And scatters night away*

"I was almost four," Cash recalled, "but I remember the ice hanging off the trees. It was raining and freezing all the way up. We found house No. 266 and moved in. All us kids slept on the floor that night."[2]

Daddy Cash and Johnny's oldest brother cleared ten acres that first year and planted their first cottonseeds. They also caught water moccasins and wildcats and used the hides for floor coverings and makeshift mattresses for the smaller Cash kids. In those days a decent cotton crop brought two bales to the acre. "Dyess Colony was our salvation," Cash said. "I don't know what we would have done otherwise. Probably been following the wheat crop and going to the dogs like the others."[3]

*No chilling winds or poisonous breath*
*Can reach that healthful shore;*
*Sickness and sorrow, pain and death,*
*Are felt and feared no more*

*When I shall reach that happy place,*
*I'd be forever blest,*
*For I shall see my Father's face,*
*And in His bosom rest*

*Filled with delight my raptured soul*
*Would here no longer stay;*
*Though Jordan's waves around me roll,*
*Fearless I'd launch away*

But there were no guarantees on the new Cash homestead, either. Their new start on the Delta didn't necessarily mean outside forces never worked against them—forces like the Mississippi River. In fact, one of Cash's many storied tunes—"Five Feet High and Rising"—came from seeing with his own eyes how unstoppable acts of nature could destroy months of backbreaking work in the cotton fields, not to mention their still meager income.

"I remember when I was a kid about five years old one mornin' in 1937—the winter of 1937," Cash said to a concert audience years later, "the rain had been fallin' day and night, and all the old folks kept sayin' yes, if that river keeps risin' it's goin' to break that levee and come right over that cotton land. One mornin' the Mississippi River broke the levee at Wilson, Arkansas, and I woke up and that black, muddy Mississippi River water was right up to the front door, and I heard my daddy holler and ask my momma, 'How high's the water, momma?' 'Two feet high and risin',' she answered."[4]

Even in his last days, with his weak, seventy-one-year-old frame, he was still broad shouldered and gifted with strong hands—and that's due in large part to all his hard labor in the cotton fields, a backbreaking chore that began much earlier for Cash than for his siblings. He'd eventually work up to 350 pounds of picked cotton a day. "John was probably the only one of us kids who worked on the farm and didn't complain," sister Reba said.[5]

Well, maybe he didn't complain then—and certainly not to anyone's face. But later in life, he unchained his disdain for his childhood labors: "The hardest thing I ever did in my life? Hell, that's easy: cotton ... I picked it, I chopped it, I hauled it. It was drudgery."[6,7]

When he wasn't scarring his young fingers in the fields and bagging hundreds of pounds of cotton, Cash could sometimes be found in the clothing section of the local store—not that he or his folks ever purchased much to wear. "When you know you can't have things, you don't want for them," he reasoned. "I always got something to eat when I was hungry, and the rest didn't bother me.[8]

"I never have been all the way down and out," Cash said. "I've been down physically and mentally at times, so I understand what it's like to feel like an underdog ... When I was a little kid I'd hunt rabbits and squirrels simply because we needed them to eat, and they were really good. If my daddy gave me two shells, I was supposed to bring back two rabbits. I'm still like that. I go rabbit hunting and I won't take but two shells."[9]

When there weren't freshly killed rabbits to eat, "sometimes at supper we had to fill up on turnip greens, and sometimes at breakfast it was just flapjacks and biscuits—but that was plenty."[10]

Regardless of what was on the table, the Cashes gave thanks to God before every meal. It wasn't an empty ritual, either—the Cash family was truly grateful, even for just the will and muscle to get through the day and earn enough to keep their hungry mouths fed.[11] Their Baptist heritage ran deep in their veins, after all. (Cash's grandpa and great-grandpa were missionary Baptist preachers, and two of his great-uncles were Baptist preachers as well.)

Said Carrie Rivers Cash, "We raised all our children up to be good Christian children. They're all members of churches. They may have strayed—but not far."[12]

## THAT OLD TIME RELIGION

While the Cashes were relieved to have a roof over their heads and their daddy at home on a consistent basis, the next step was figuring out how they fit into their new community. "We had no recreation hall in Dyess," Reba said, "and really about the only thing we had was our school activities and church. We were very active in church."[13]

Joanne Yates, another of Cash's sisters, noted that the family split time between the local Baptist church—which had some "great congregational singing"—and then headed down to the local Pentecostal church.

"Sometimes we'd get scared to death in church," Yates remembered. "The preacher preached hellfire and brimstone … We sang some of the same old songs that are still around, like 'Amazing Grace' and 'Unclouded Day.'"[14]

The Road Fifteen Church of God met in an aged schoolhouse. And even though she was raised Methodist and wasn't a member of Road Fifteen, Cash's momma loved their services and regularly brought young J.R. along.

Like his sister's memories, Cash's recollections aren't the happiest.

"The thing I remember most was fear," Cash recalled. "I didn't understand it as worship then. I only knew it was some place momma was making me go with her. The preacher terrified me. He shouted and cried and gasped … But the people were caught up in the fever. The preacher would walk into the congregation and grab someone up out of their seat, shouting, 'Come to God! Repent!' And he'd lead them to the altar where they'd fall to their knees … The writhing on the floor, the moaning, the trembling, and the jerks they got into scared me even more. And the preacher standing over a woman lying on the floor sweating and shouting, 'Hallelujah! Praise God! Praise God!'"[15]

For J.R., there was no joy in witnessing these strange scenes—to him all the crying and carrying on meant these folks were in pain. Yet somehow his momma left those services with a happy countenance and peace he couldn't fathom.[16]

But after a while the Gospel message he heard every week began to sink in. By the time Cash reached ten or eleven—not quite the "age of accountability," in his mind—he knew there were two definite paths he could travel in life, and he wanted to get his heart right with God. He had observed those who made that fateful choice for the light, and they were very different from "the ones playing checkers over at the service station during the church service."[17]

Just after he reached his twelfth birthday, Cash felt a stirring in his heart one night during a revival meeting. Cash was rapt as the preacher went through his sermon ... and then the first notes of the invitational song rang out. It was a tune Cash would eventually record in 1975, the title of which adorns a special collection of his favorite spiritual songs:[18]

*Just as I am, without one plea,*
*But that Thy blood was shed for me,*
*And that Thou bidst me come to Thee,*
*O Lamb of God, I come, I come*

"It was not that I had been such a bad boy," Cash remembered. "It was just that the right way and the wrong way had been laid down to me so surely by my parents ... The necessity of my making a choice was inevitable. If I did not accept Christ, I was rejecting Him, and I knew who Jesus was and why He'd come ... I understood, and I believed. I needed Him as my Savior in order to become an heir of heaven."[19]

*Just as I am, and waiting not*
*To rid my soul of one dark blot,*
*To Thee whose blood can cleanse each spot,*

*O Lamb of God, I come, I come*

"I finally got up the courage to step out of that pew, walk down the aisle, and take the preacher's hand," Cash recalled. "There was not any big burst of shouting or fireworks, but a beautiful peace came over me that night. And a relief that I had stepped out and chosen the way that had been pointed out to me all those years."[20]

*Just as I am, though tossed about*
*With many a conflict, many a doubt,*
*Fightings and fears within, without,*
*O Lamb of God, I come, I come.*

## ABBA, FATHER ...

While Cash's newfound spiritual anchor was taking root in his life, things weren't always peaceful at home.

Sometimes Ray Cash came home drunk—and that meant anything could happen. One morning Johnny heard him yelling and swearing at his momma, not letting her answer him back, until he finally announced that he was going to wallop her.

Then the unbelievable happened.

His older brother Jack stopped his dangerously drunk—and much larger—father. Jack stepped between his momma and daddy and yelled at Ray Cash that he'd have to hit him first. Incredibly, the elder Cash backed off.

Then there was the time his daddy killed young J.R.'s beloved dog, Jake Terry, a stray that he spotted heading down the road into town and brought home. One day J.R. came home from school and called Jake Terry, but he didn't come. So he and Jack went looking for him—but not before asking their daddy if he'd seen him.

"No," he said.

But J.R. and Jack found the dog at the far end of the cotton rows across a shallow ditch with a .22 bullet in his skull.

Again, Jack confronted Ray Cash: "We found Jake Terry down there across the ditch."

The elder Cash replied, "Yeah, I killed him. I didn't want to have to tell you boys, but we just didn't need another dog around here." (The Cashes already had a dog named Ray.)[21]

Many years later, Ray Cash was a bit more repentant. "I wouldn't have killed that dog if I'd have thought about it," he said. "I hated the killing, but it was done."[22]

J.R.—who was five years old at the time—was devastated. "I thought my world had ended that morning, that nothing was safe, that life wasn't safe," he recalled. "It was a frightening thing, and it took a long time for me to get over it. It was a cut that went deep and stayed there."[23]

While Ray Cash wasn't a complete ogre, it's safe to say that Cash had a love-hate relationship with his father. And while the elder Cash's often dismissive attitude regarding J.R.'s needs and dreams (especially musical) was a tough row to hoe, he was able to tough it out and get through his childhood. There was a lot missing, though.

"[My father] never once told me he loved me, and he never had a loving hand to lay on his children," Cash noted. "He said once that he didn't have to tell people he loved them for them to know it, and perhaps that was true. Still, it would have meant an awful lot for me to have heard it, just once, before he died."[24]

## PEERING OVER THE HORIZON

One day in 1936, with money coming into the Cash household on a more regular basis, the clan splurged for a battery radio—electricity would not reach their home for another decade—and the strains of embryonic country music on Friday and Saturday nights from the Grand Ole Opry felt like honey in J.R.'s ears. The gadget added fuel to the fire building in his soul.[25]

At that point Cash began hoping for options beyond life on a cotton farm.

And while Cash's parents and the church fed him a healthy dose of old-fashioned virtues throughout his childhood—industriousness, thrift, honesty, and religious zeal weren't in short supply—their frequently confining requirements more than likely led Cash down a road that, for a long while, didn't actively include God.

As author Christopher S. Wren pointed out, "they were bound to constrict, breeding within Cash a latent restlessness that would erupt into rebellion years later."[26]

CHAPTER TWO

# CAN YOU HEAR THE ANGELS?

*"As a child, I dreamed an angel came … to tell me my brother Jack would die, but that I must understand that it was God's plan, and someday I would see that it was. Jack died two weeks later."*[1]

PUT SIMPLY, JOHNNY CASH IDOLIZED his big brother, Jack.

"I really admired him … respected him. He was a very mature person for his age, thoughtful and reliable and steady. There was such substance to him—such seriousness, if you like, or even moral weight, such gravitas—that when he made it known that he'd felt a call from God to be a minister of the Gospel, nobody ever thought to question either his sincerity or the legitimacy of his decision."[2]

To most others who encountered him, Jack Cash was a marvel, a little tower of physical and spiritual strength unlike anyone else they ever saw before or since. Still a youth, he not only regularly called adults (like his father) on their heinous behavior, it seemed Jack could literally rise above just about any adverse situation.

Cash recalled a confrontation he witnessed between Jack and a spiteful storeowner in Dyess who belonged to a branch of Christianity that believed their "truth" was exclusive. Out of nowhere, the man yelled, "Jack, you know if you don't belong to my church you're going to hell, don't you?" Unfazed, Jack looked at the man, smiled, and began singing:

*Have you been to Jesus for the cleansing power,*
*Are you washed in the blood of the Lamb?*
*Are you fully trusting in His grace this hour*
*Are you washed in the blood of the Lamb?*

Upon hearing Jack intone "Are You Washed in the Blood?" the man's face became flushed, he threw down his butcher's knife, and turned his back on the two brothers.[3]

Despite Cash's admiration for Jack, it didn't necessarily lead to emulation, however. In many ways, the brothers couldn't be more different. While young J.R. was weak, scrawny, and skinny, Jack—though only two years older—was strong and powerfully built for his age. What's more, about the same time J.R. accepted Jesus into his life, he also developed a taste for cigarettes—a taste of things to come for this youthful walking contradiction. Cash would lift tobacco from Daddy, bum the occasional cigarette from older kids, and when the money was there, he'd sometimes purchase a pack of his own tobacco and roll 'em himself.[4]

"Even back then, no matter what older folks say now, everybody knew smoking hurt you," Cash said. "But I've never been one to let such considerations stand in the way of my road to ruin. Jack knew I smoked and didn't approve one bit, but he didn't criticize me. Putting it in today's terms, he gave me unconditional love."[5]

## MAY 12, 1944

It was a Saturday morning, and Cash had fishing on his mind. He hoped Jack would join him, but Jack's mind was on making extra money for the family—he worked a table saw at the high school agricultural shop where he cut oak trees into fence posts. But something felt strange from the very start of the day.[6]

Cash remembered his momma saying, "Jack, you seem like you don't feel you should go."

"I don't," he replied, "I feel like something's going to happen."[7]

She pleaded with him to stay. J.R. did as well.

"Go fishing with me, Jack," Cash said. "Come on, let's go fishing." But Jack was adamant, despite the almost tangible sense of resignation and sadness in his movements toward the front door. No words were spoken—but Carrie Cash watched her sons head away from the house. That was strange, too, Cash thought—she never did that.

What's more, the usually serious and straightforward Jack was acting weird. While J.R. continued to plead with him to skip work and go fishing, Jack responded by imitating a relatively new cartoon character: "What's up, doc? What's up, doc?" Jack cackled in the midst of his younger brother's growing alarm.

"[So] I went on down toward our fishing hole," Cash remembered. "As long as I could hear him, he kept up with that goofy, unnatural, 'What's up, doc? What's up, doc?'"[8]

At the fishing hole, things didn't feel better—only worse. Cash, now all alone, sensed something was amiss, but he couldn't figure out what it was. A few hours later, he picked up his rod and headed toward home—and that's when he saw his daddy in their old Model A car barreling down the road.

Ray Cash told J.R. to throw his fishing rod in the ditch and jump inside—fast. The elder Cash was clearly upset. Something was terribly wrong.

"Jack's been hurt really bad," Ray Cash said.[9]

When Ray Cash and J.R. got back home, his daddy pulled a brown paper bag from the back of the car and told J.R. to follow him into the smokehouse—he had something to show him.

It was a bloody pile of clothes. Jack's clothes.

Turns out that while Jack was working the table saw, he got caught and was pulled across the table. The blade sliced him wide open from his ribcage to his groin. Nobody figured Jack had a chance.

"We did see Jack alive," Cash remembered. "He was unconscious when we got to the hospital, knocked out with drugs for the pain, but he didn't go right ahead and die. On Wednesday, four days after he'd been hurt, all the church congregations in town held a special service for him, and the following morning he had an amazing revival. He said he felt good, and he looked good. There he was, fine as you please, lying in bed reading his mail—he'd gotten a letter from his girlfriend—and laughing happily. My mother and father and I thought we were seeing a miracle, Jack was going to live!"[10]

It was not to be. Eight days after the accident, Cash woke from a deep sleep hearing the sound of his daddy crying and praying—something he'd never seen before. When he saw J.R. awake, he suggested they go into Jack's room and say goodbye.

Carrie Cash, Ray, and all of J.R.'s brothers and sisters were gathered around Jack's bed, crying. At first, Jack was delirious: "The mules are out, don't let 'em get in the corn, catch the mules!" Then he got quiet and calm … and looked around at his family. "I'm glad you're all here," he said.

Then he shut his eyes. "It's a beautiful river," he said. "It's going two ways … No I'm not going that way … Yes, that's the way I'm going … Aaaaw, Momma, can't you see it?"

"No, son, I can't see it," she said.

"Well, can you hear the angels?"

"No, son, I can't hear the angels."

Jack started crying. "I wish you could," he said. "It's so wonderful, and what a beautiful place that I'm going."

Then he was gone.[11]

## PICKING UP THE PIECES

"He was a child of God. A man-child. Wisdom beyond his years," June Carter Cash wrote in her 1987 book, *From the Heart*. "He did not know hate—it passed him by—and you wonder how I know him when I never met him. It took him fourteen years to die. You see I know his brother well. I lie with him at night. He shivers in his dreams and sometimes calls for Jack, but the angels sung a louder song, and Jack ain't coming back. I know Jack was good, kind, and pure. He left ahead of time, John tells me as he weeps. There's no way for him to know how I know Jack so well. John tells me when he sleeps."[12]

Losing his older brother was a tragedy that Cash never really completely recovered from. "It's still a big, cold, sad place in my heart and soul. After Jack's death I felt like I'd died, too. I just didn't feel alive. I was terribly lonely without him. I had no other friend."[13]

He became very quiet, not uttering many words for almost a year after Jack died. "It's the toughest thing to do, seeing your brother go," Cash noted during a CMT network interview. "It made me ask, 'Where do we all stand with God?'"

And even though their collective devastation hadn't come close to running its course, the Cashes went back to their work in the fields the day after Jack's funeral. But the monotony of their labors couldn't numb their pain. J.R. saw his momma fall to her knees and watched her head droop to her chest. Ray Cash quickly rushed over and took her by the arm, but Carrie Cash refused his aid.

"I'll get up when God pushes me up!" she said, angrily and desperately. "And soon she was on her feet working with her hoe."[14]

If enduring the grief itself wasn't enough for the Cashes, Johnny later pointed to a rarely discussed, contentious issue surrounding Jack's death.

"It was an accident only 'in the family's mind.' It was murder," he once told an interviewer, speaking slowly and uncomfortably. "There was a neighbor that went down to the shop with him that day and disappeared after the accident. We couldn't prove anything, but I always thought of it as murder. My mother and daddy didn't. They never mentioned that boy. Nothin' was ever done about it."[15]

## DADDY TURNS AROUND

After Jack died, Ray Cash declared his faith in Jesus. He quit drinking, too. In the following year, he became a deacon of the church. Once he was even called to preach during the pastor's absence and responded by saying, "You've called on me to preach today, and I can't turn you down, but I don't deserve to be here. I'm an evil man. I always have been. I don't deserve to stand in this pulpit."[16]

But he was apparently no slouch there. The passage he read was from 2 Chronicles: "If my people, which are called by My name, shall humble themselves and pray and seek My face and turn from their wicked ways, then I will hear from heaven and will forgive their sin and will heal their land." Ray Cash didn't yell, something J.R. likely expected given his track record. Instead he was cool and in control. "I was impressed," Cash said later, "and I think the congregation was, too. It was such a wonderful thing for me, seeing him in the pulpit."[17]

## UNLESS A GRAIN OF WHEAT FALLS ...

According to Cash's sister Joanne, the day Jack died was a major turning for Cash's own fledgling faith—and the power of that day eventually helped spark his return many years later to the Christian teachings he once esteemed in Dyess.

"Jack was John's next oldest brother, and John nearly worshiped him," Joanne noted. "Jack was always very spiritual-minded, much more than the rest of us. John didn't get over [his death] for years; he was terribly shook up—and I think he made a kind of silent promise to Jack when he was dying ... Now John has come back to God, and I think he's finally fulfilled a promise to Jack. Last night we were in the studio recording 'Amazing Grace' with the church choir. I looked over at him, and he was closing his eyes to hide the tears while he sang along with us. I couldn't help but think then, 'The whole choir may be singing to God, but I believe John is singing back to Jack.'"[18]

Cash later affirmed that Jack's influence on him remained profound—and, in that sense, he really remained not so far away.

"When we were kids he tried to turn me from the way of death to the way of life, to steer me toward the light," Cash said, "and since he died his words and his example have been like signposts for me. The most important question in many of the conundrums and crises of my life has been, 'Which is

Jack's way? Which direction would he have taken?'" And even during his lowest, most pitiful moments of drug abuse and failing health, Cash believed Jack's voice was always audible in his soul—a kind of virtuous fly in the ruinous ointment Cash continually spread on himself.[19]

Cash always noted that he felt Jack's presence in the songs for his funeral—"Peace in the Valley," "I'll Fly Away," "How Beautiful Heaven Must Be"—and that even more, those songs have sustained and renewed him throughout his life. "Wherever I go, I can start singing one of them and immediately begin to feel peace settle over me as God's grace flows in. At times they've been my only way back, the only door out of the dark, bad places the black dog calls home."[20]

Jack showed up in Cash's dreams as well—he's made appearances there ever since his death, even aging and growing up with Cash. "Jack is always two years older than me," he explained. "When I was 20, he was 22 … and the last time I saw him, about three weeks ago, his hair was gray and his beard was snowy white. He's a preacher, just as he intended to be, a good man and a figure of high repute. He's still wise, too. Usually in my Jack dreams I'm having some sort of problem or I'm doing something questionable, and I'll notice him looking at me, smiling, as if to say, 'I know you, J.R. I know what you've really got in your mind … .' There's no fooling Jack."[21]

CHAPTER THREE

# GOD'S GOT HIS HAND ON YOU

DURING HIS GROWING UP YEARS, SINGING was pretty much as natural as breathing for young J.R. Cash. He sang everywhere, all the time.

"Songs were my life," he recalled in 2002. "I feasted on them."[1]

He sang in church: "John sang in the choir, but he also sang special pieces," his sister Reba noted. "He had a boy soprano voice when he was younger. Then it dropped all of a sudden. He never went through a croaky stage."[2]

He sang in the cotton fields: "I did some of my best singing when I was plowing," Cash said. "And some of my loudest. I had a very high voice, a high tenor, and I'd yodel."[3]

He sang walking down the road: "The long walk home at night was scary," Cash remembered. "It was pitch dark on the gravel road, and if the moon was shining, the shadows were even scarier ... and I just knew that in every dark spot on the road was a cottonmouth snake ready to kill me. But I sang all the way home ... and with the imaginary sound of the Gibson acoustic ... I decided that kind of music was going to be my magic to take me through all the dark places."[4]

And to prevent his daddy from catching him staying up past bedtime, Cash also sang late at night with the radio barely whispering country hits. Once Ray Cash asked J.R. why he spent so much time listening to music on the radio—"It ain't real, it's just a record," his daddy insisted.

"I don't care," J.R. replied. "It sounds good. I like it."

"Well, you're getting sucked in by all them people," Ray Cash said sternly. "That's going to keep you from making a living. You'll never do anything good as long as you've got that music on your mind."

While J.R. was hurt by his daddy's latest discouraging words, it lit a fire in his belly. "I badly wanted to prove him wrong."[5]

So—shortly after Jack died—J.R. began writing songs. He'd improvise them in front of his friends and also compose poetic lyrics when he was by himself. Much to Ray Cash's chagrin (if he knew at all), J.R. would scour ads in country music magazines that promised fame and fortune if you would send in tunes—which Cash did, quite a few times. "Then they started sending me the feeders," he recalled. "They didn't get any of my money though, because I couldn't raise it."[6]

While Daddy Cash had no love for music on the radio, he and his family absolutely loved making music themselves at home. And J.R. wasn't the only Cash to sing while toiling in the cotton fields; when the sun began settling down for the night, the Cashes would often intone slower spirituals, ending the day's work with "Life's Evening Sun Is Sinking Low." What's more, the Cashes would never fail to sing all the songs that adorned Jack's funeral service.[7]

Once indoors, sometimes Ray Cash sat at the family piano improvising chords while the rest of the clan belted out old hymns. The Baptist hymns were as close to their souls as old friends on the farm. Music and religion were the twin pillars of the Cash household—and young J.R. didn't know one without the other, so tightly were they intertwined.[8]

"The music in the Pentecostal churches in the early years was just wonderful," Cash wrote in the liner notes to his *Unchained* album. "They were more liberal with the musical instruments used. I learned to sit through the scary sermon, just to hear the music: mandolins, fiddles, bass, banjo, and flattop guitars. Hell might be on the horizon, but the wonderful gospel-spiritual songs carried me above it."

Of all of Cash's relatives, his momma was the one who instilled in him an active love and interest in music. "She could play guitar, and fiddle, too, and she sang well. The first singing I remember was hers ... I was about four years old, sitting on a chair right beside her on the front porch. She'd sing, *What would you give*—and I'd chime right in with my part, continuing the line—*in exchange for your soul?*"[9]

Carrie Cash recognized that music was in J.R.'s soul just as it was in hers—and as it had been in her father's, who was an expert four-part harmony singer and the hymn leader in his church. (Cash's grandfather, it was said, was good enough to make it as a professional singer. In fact, fans of his traveled far and wide to hear him sing.)[10]

Not only that, but Momma Cash had faith in J.R.—so much that she sweated over schoolteachers' laundry to pay for singing lessons for him. She washed and ironed a pair of pants and half a dozen shirts from midnight to 1 a.m.—not an easy task as Carrie Cash toiled on a scrub board and a makeshift ironing board. Her pay? One dollar. But she knew J.R. needed half of that just for a thirty-minute lesson.

Cash was (of course) aghast that she would spend so much needed money on a voice coach. At first he refused—but Momma won the day (of course), and Cash was soon heading for his first singing lesson.[11]

## "DON'T LET ME OR ANYONE ELSE CHANGE THE WAY YOU SING"

The sessions with Miss Mae Fielder were, at first, uneventful.

But during his third lesson—with Fielder playing piano and J.R. singing old Irish ballads such as "Drink to Me Only with Thine Eyes" and "I'll Take You Home Again Kathleen"—she stopped and said she wanted Cash to sing to her "what you like to sing," without accompaniment. With that, Cash aired out Hank Williams' "Long Gone Lonesome Blues."

"When I was through she said, 'Don't ever take voice lessons again. Don't let me or anyone else change the way you sing.' The she sent me home.[12]

"Then one day—I was 18—I came in from cutting wood. Momma was cooking supper and I sang: *Everybody gonna have religion and glory / Everybody gonna be singing this story*.

"Momma turned around. 'Who was that?' she said.

"I said, 'That was me Momma.'

"I was really hitting those low notes. Boy, I was so proud I didn't shut up for days."[13]

Cash sang more songs for his momma, exploring his new, lower, richer range. And when he went for it, exploring just how low he could now take his new baritone, Carrie Cash's eyes teared up. "You sound exactly like my daddy. God has His hand on you, son. Don't ever forget the gift. You'll be singing for the world someday."

That was the first time Cash heard his momma referring to his voice as "the gift," but she used those words from then on anytime she talked about his music. "I think she did so on purpose," Cash remembered, "to remind me that the music in me was something special given by God. My job was to care for it and use it well; I was its bearer, not its owner."[14]

Cash didn't do much public singing at that point, save for a few school functions here and there. During a school singing contest, though, Cash won five dollars for his rendition of "That Lucky Old Sun (Just Rolls Around Heaven All Day)," after which he went out and purchased a brand new pair of pants. (Near the end of his life he would record the same song—under very different financial circumstances.) Now that he knew he could earn money from working in country music, Cash's appetite for the world of music became stronger and stronger.

Interestingly, it was his momma who understood before anybody else that his musical talent could also lead to his downfall.

"He was so good that Momma used to worry about him getting into music and leaving the Lord," Cash's sister Joanne recalled. "Nobody knows how many times she spent the night on her knees in prayer for him. In the days when things were going bad for him, all the press reports of the trouble he was in really hurt Momma. She read the papers and worried and prayed for him constantly."[15]

Aside from his singing, Cash's high school experience wasn't terribly indicative of what was to come. Academically, he performed pretty badly during his freshman year, receiving Cs and Ds mostly—save for a few Bs toward the end of the school year. But by his senior year, Cash was mostly Bs all the way. Unsurprisingly, he did best in the classes he liked the best—and they were invariably English and history. Aside from that, Cash at one time or another was part of several student organizations, including the 4-H Club, the Boy Scouts, and the Future Farmers of America. He was even growing out of his scrawniness, playing some basketball and—drum roll, please—winning an Arkansas Boys State swimming championship by the time his eighteenth birthday rolled around.[16]

But there was a poignant moment during those years that proved a portent of life-changing events to come: It happened on a class trip to Nashville and the Grand Ole Opry—Cash first laid eyes on June Carter.

(Six years later he saw her perform again and somehow weaseled his way backstage to meet her in person. Incredibly Cash blurted out, "You and I are going to get married some day." June didn't jump ship from her husband right then and there—Cash himself was married at the time, too—but she was intrigued.)

Through all these slow-building experiences, Carrie Cash's words always rang hard and heavy in her son's head: Don't forget the gift. God's got His hand on you. Don't forget the gift. God's got His hand on you ...

But first, Cash had to get out of Dyess.

CHAPTER FOUR

# WANDERLUST WHETTED

WHEN THE TWENTIETH CENTURY HIT THE halfway point—when pundits made their obligatory predictions about what would change the world between 1950 and the start of the new millennium—Johnny Cash graduated from high school. (Think they predicted somebody like him would come along?)

As with many high school grads, the moment Cash received his diploma was the green light to leave home. But it wasn't terribly easy going. Without the money to attend college or the confidence or experience yet to launch a music career, he didn't know exactly what he wanted to do. There wasn't any money in staying on his family's farm, as Ray Cash had rented out the cotton patches and taken work elsewhere.

He did hear that the strawberry picking was pretty good in nearby Bald Knob. A family from Dyess he knew was doing just that—maybe he could stay with them? No such luck.

After a hitchhiking trek, not only was there no bed for Cash to sleep in (he bunked in the woodshed), the strawberries were scarce. He made three bucks over three miserable days. Not the greatest start to his adult life.

Upon returning to Dyess, Cash got wind of young men from town who traveled north to find higher-paying employment in automobile factories. So up north he went, taking a train, then a Greyhound bus, to Detroit. A far cry from the banks of the Mississippi, indeed.

Cash settled in a boarding house in Pontiac, Michigan, with a bunch of other guys his age from Dyess. But the presence of familiar faces didn't quell his distaste for the drudgery of the punch-press job that demanded he rise at 4:30 a.m. and walk a mile and half to the Fisher Body plant. His already skinny frame (6 feet, 2 inches tall; 150 pounds) withered by ten pounds in two weeks. He got sick. Then after cutting his arm on a car hood, Cash quit and hitchhiked back to Dyess.

His growing wanderlust whetted, the moment of truth had arrived. He needed to do something with his life, and he couldn't make it happen in Dyess or Detroit. So, on July 7, 1950, Cash signed up for a four-year stint with the United States Air Force.[1]

## BASIC TRAINING

With no real hope for flying the coop again, Cash quickly settled into his new life as a soldier on Lackland Air Force Base in San Antonio, Texas. Though it was technically the South, San Antonio might as well have been Detroit—it wasn't the homey Dyess to which he'd grown so accustomed.

He longed for something else, too.

"I really missed singing with everyone in church," Cash noted, significantly. "But marching music was fun, too. I still remember the first song we sang that way, a group effort written collaboratively by my whole flight of fifty-seven men and sung on the march."[2]

More and more, his old hometown and his old church—and all the good, upright, moral instruction he received growing up there—were becoming a blip on Cash's radar screen. He even changed the name he grew up with (J.R.) to John, after his superiors required a more conventional first name from him—so that part of Cash was gone, too. His letters home slowed down, and before long they stopped altogether.

"I guess I started to be a fairly profane person," Cash noted, "because for the first time in my life I got to seeing how good I could curse."[3] Thus began his slow, painful trek into the spiritual wilderness.

## ON THE RADIO

With basic training nearing its end, Cash had another decision to make—choice of duty. His options were air police, aircraft mechanic, and radio operator. Since he demonstrated promising potential in communications, Cash set his sights on the latter and began six months of training at Mississippi's Keesler Air Force Base.

That's when good things finally started happening.

He got the hang of Morse Code so quickly that he finished his class four weeks early—well ahead of his fellow students. His instructors were duly impressed and chose Cash as a candidate for the USAF Security Service.

And for the first time since he revealed his magical baritone for his momma, Cash found something else he excelled at. His security service training was no picnic, however. Cash was going head to head with university graduates who stood a much better chance than Cash of learning this new, complex technology. It was survival of the fittest, as only a handful of the most qualified students would make the cut—but Cash had a wildcard: In high school, he wisely made the decision to learn the touch-typing technique—not necessarily a "guy thing" in the late 1940s. But his unconventional skill turned into a major advantage: "They kept us going for eight hours a day on simulated coded broadcasts, at thirty or thirty-five words per minute," Cash said. "I got so I could copy over forty words per minute. I could copy Morse Code faster on a typewriter than I could type regularly."[4]

Cash got the gig, and soon he was headed overseas for the first time ever: Landsberg, Germany, a million miles away from Arkansas in his heart and mind—and supremely exciting and invigorating. Plus, he made fast friends with a handful of barracks mates who, like Cash, were country music fans—these guys even played guitar and sang. They'd sit around and rake out tunes by the likes of the Carter Family, Hank Williams, Jimmie Rodgers, Roy Acuff, Ernest Tubb, and Hank Snow. They formed a fun-loving gang, the "Landsberg Barbarians." And given their frequent descents into all sorts of hijinks in civilian taverns and beer gardens—where they also played their guitars and mandolins for the feverish locals—the band moniker was fitting.[5]

After tasting many times how good the music sounded and felt, Cash visited a Landsberg music store and paid twenty deutschemarks (then about five dollars) for a new acoustic. He walked out of the store with his first six-string ever in the middle of a snowstorm—a first-time musical experience not unlike the freezing midwinter drive to Dyess when he heard his first gospel song, "I Am Bound for the Promised Land."

This time, though, Cash's promised land was nowhere near a cotton field.

With his guitar now a constant companion, Cash learned the instrument quickly and was soon accompanying himself. Incredibly, he composed one of his best-known songs, "Folsom Prison Blues," on base after watching an eye-opening film about prison conditions called *Inside the Walls of Folsom Prison*. The famously sinister verse, *I shot a man in Reno just to watch him die* was the result, he later wrote, of "trying to think up the worst reason a person could have for killing another person."[6]

"I was so lonely for those three years [in the Air Force]," Cash admitted in 1996. "If I couldn't have sung all those old country songs, I don't think I could have made it."[7]

Despite his bouts of loneliness, Cash's life in Landsberg was a rush of discovery and growth. Still, there were ugly moments, too. Racial tension that existed in the barracks often turned violent. Something Cash couldn't understand. "I had no problem sharing a barracks with blacks," Cash stated later, "and I couldn't imagine hating them so much that I was willing to wage a private war on them. It's quite a thing, the innocence of youth; my views haven't changed since then, but I've certainly learned more about race hatred along the way."[8]

## WEDDING BELLS

When Cash hit American soil as an honorably discharged Air Force sergeant on July 4, 1954, two major things were on his mind: The first was getting hitched to Vivian Liberto, a young woman he met at a roller rink in Texas only two weeks before shipping out to Germany. (The two stayed in close touch, developing a relationship via daily doses of mail.) The second goal in Cash's mind was launching a singing career. Liberto was supportive of his desires—even the musical dreams.

"The only singing she'd heard me do was on a disk I'd make in a booth at the railroad station in Munich for one deutsche mark—my first record, an unaccompanied rendition of 'Am I the One?' She wore it out," Cash said, acknowledging the sad irony in verse, *Am I the one who'll always hold you, 'til the end of time …* The song was composed by Carl Smith—June Carter's husband at the time.[9]

Significantly, Cash admitted that his spiritual path took some odd turns after he married Vivian, a devoted Catholic girl. Following their move to Memphis, Cash took a suggestion from his father-in-law and enrolled in a six-month class in basic Catholicism taught by a local priest. But that concession didn't help bridge the spiritual gulf between the couple—Cash continued to drive Vivian to Catholic services at 9 a.m., then headed off by his lonesome to a Protestant service at 10:30 a.m.[10]

But Cash managed to find solace in the music that seemed to seep from Memphis' every pore. The blues were everywhere. Cash was a regular visitor to the record store, Home of the Blues, where he purchased *Blues in the Mississippi Night*, a collection of tunes by obscure Delta blues singers—one of

Cash's all-time favorite albums. He also headed into the black part of town, Orange Mound, and hung around the front porch of singer/songwriter Gus Cannon, listening to him belt out his tunes in person. (Cannon wrote "Walk Right In," a pop hit for an outfit called the Rooftop Singers.) Cash also took in "Red Hot and Blue," Dewey Philip's radio show on WHBQ. On his program, genres got melded together—hillbilly, pop, blues, and gospel all got a fair hearing—and Cash got his first taste of musical barrier breaking.[11]

But with a wife to support, Cash couldn't spend all his time daydreaming about making it big—he had to make money, too. He considered taking a job with the Memphis police, but settled on a door-to-door sales gig pitching used washing machines.

"Oh, it was a hard job, and I hated every minute of it," Cash revealed. "I'd go down to the poorest sections of town, but I might as well have told them, 'You don't want to buy anything anyway.' I'd be in a home and I'd see a guitar, and I'd sit and play and forget the business."[12]

## BIRTH OF A LEGENDARY BAND

Cash's eldest brother, Roy, was night-service manager of an automobile sales garage in town, and he coaxed Johnny out to the shop one day. Knowing his kid brother's affinity for music, Roy figured it couldn't hurt to introduce Johnny to a couple of the mechanics there—Marshall Grant and Luther Perkins.

Grant was the day-service manager, and Perkins was a magician with generators, starters, and voltage regulators. More importantly, like Cash, they both played guitar. Near suppertime, if jobs were slow going, Grant and Perkins often headed to the back of the shop and strummed and picked. Sometimes after work they'd hit Roy's house, too, and jam for hours.[13]

"Before I ever shook his hand, before I ever spoke to him, I saw him coming down the rows of cars, and he seemed almost magnetic," said Grant of his first meeting with Cash. "Even though he was just J.R. then, there was something that caught your attention. He was tall and dark, and he was as edgy as a cat on a tin roof. It was a pretty warm day, and he was drenched with perspiration. He was that way near every time I saw him for a couple of years."[14]

Cash joined Marshall and Perkins' informal jam sessions, and things began moving quickly. Cash had the voice and immediately began leading the trio. Marshall switched to upright bass and learned it lickity split; Perkins stayed on guitar, but sprung for an electric. But playing for each other would get them nowhere—they needed an audience.

Fortunately for Cash, his boss at Home Equipment—George Bates—was "one of those angels who appear in your life just when you need them, holding out a hand to you in the right place at the right time."[15]

After making twenty dollars a week for about the fifth week in a row, Bates called Cash in and asked him point-blank what he really wanted to do. Cash said he wanted to sing on the radio and make records. Instead of dismissing the young singer like Ray Cash did years before, Bates asked what it would take to get him on the radio. Cash replied that he'd need a sponsor—and that the cost was fifteen dollars for a fifteen-minute show. Bates told Cash that Home Equipment would sponsor him and his fledgling outfit.[16]

So they got their slot playing gospel numbers from 2 to 2:15 p.m. on KWEM every Saturday. That's how the spare, sparse, no-frills sound produced by Cash, Perkins, and Grant—soon to be known as Johnny Cash and the Tennessee Two—became a known oddity in the belly of country music.

Their weekly residency also spawned live dates for the fledgling band. Their very first was a performance at a North Memphis church. Other dates were mostly in movie theaters during intermissions, high school auditoriums, or grassy ballparks—never bars or taverns, as Cash refused to mix music and alcohol.[17] As with their radio show, their live gigs consisted of mostly gospel material—"Peace in the Valley," "He'll Understand and Say Well Done," even Black gospel blues such as "I've Got Jesus and That's Enough," and without fail, "I Was There When It Happened." Cash also pulled out a tune he recently wrote called "Belshazzar":[18] *For he was weighed in the balance and found wanting/ His kingdom was divided, couldn't stand/ He was weighed in the balance and found wanting/ His houses were built upon the sand …* [19]

It was during their first public performance in the North Memphis church that Cash picked up a habit of wearing black-colored clothes onstage. He wanted his band to look like a band—but none of the guys had any passable stage clothes to speak of. They each did own a black shirt and blue jeans, though. That became the band's "look."

And since the church folk liked the boys—and since musicians are deeply superstitious—Cash suggested they stick with black all the time. "It still means something to me," Cash noted later. "It's still my symbol of rebellion—against a stagnant status quo, against our hypocritical houses of God, against people whose minds are closed to others' ideas."[20]

The music was happening. Cash, Grant, and Perkins were meshing as a unit. So it seemed an opportune time to take the next step. "We were still playing these little places," Grant recalled, "and one day we decided, why not go up and see if we could record at Sun?"[21]

CHAPTER FIVE

# COME ON IN!

"I DIDN'T GET DISCOVERED," CASH SAID steadfastly of his musical courtship of Sam Phillips and Sun Records in the spring of 1955. "I went down and opened the door for discovery myself."[1]

Cash's first move was a telephone call to the iconoclastic impresario, during which he told Phillips straight up that he was a gospel singer. No dice, Phillips said. No market for gospel. Can't make a living at it.

"I love gospel music," Phillips told Cash. "I love gospel singers, but I can't make money recording it. Unless you're Mahalia Jackson or somebody that established, you can't even cover the cost of recording."[2] This was disappointing to Cash, who very badly wanted to sing gospel; but he figured any foot in the door was better than being left out in the cold.

Cash's next attempt was a failure, too—he told Phillips he was a country singer. Phillips wasn't buying any of it.

"In the end I just went down to the Memphis Recording Service one morning before anyone arrived for work and sat on the step and waited," Cash explained. The first person to arrive was Phillips himself, and Cash pulled no punches: "Mr. Phillips, sir, if you listen to me, you'll be glad you did."

Bingo.

"Well, I like to hear a boy with confidence in him," Phillips replied. "Come on in!"

Finally inside the hallowed walls of Sun, Cash sang to the producer everything he liked by other artists—but Phillips was mostly interested in what he'd written. Cash told him about a new song he hadn't quite felt out completely, and Phillips said to go for it. In seconds, Cash was singing "Hey, Porter!"[3]

Bingo.

Phillips invited Cash to come back the next day with the Tennessee Two and record "Hey, Porter!" for a possible single.

Cash told Grant and Perkins the good news, but the trio was petrified upon reaching what had seemed like an impossible dream, and they were nervous in the studio the next day. But once they managed a decent take of "Hey, Porter!" Phillips was ebullient—Cash and the Tennessee Two were making a record. The song would get captured on vinyl and sent to radio stations. Yee haw!

Then Phillips wondered if Cash had other material similar to

"Hey, Porter!" Cash said he'd come up with something—Phillips wanted a "real weeper." He got just that when Cash brought in "Cry! Cry! Cry!" few weeks later.

While Cash's plea to record gospel music fell on deaf ears, he and his compadres were at least in the game—after all, there's nothing wrong with sharing label space with the likes of Elvis Presley and Roy Orbison. That was good enough for the moment.

## LESS IS MORE

Understanding exactly what Johnny Cash's early sound meant to the music community is crucial. In their own way (and with Phillips' invaluable direction), Cash, Perkins, and Grant were rockabilly revolutionaries—even if, by all standards, the trio landed nowhere near virtuoso land.

Critic Hank Davis offered this detailed analysis: "Marshall Grant played a competent string bass, and Cash's rhythm guitar was adequate. That's the good news. The rest of the story is that Luther Perkins was a remarkably limited musician. The term 'lead guitarist' doesn't really fit. But if Perkins' playing was limited, it met its match in Cash's singing. Cash's voice was deep and lonesome sounding, but it's hard to find a more restricted range in any singer of Cash's stature.

"[Yet Cash and the Tennessee Two] produced an utterly compelling ... innovative country sound. Of course, it didn't hurt that Cash wrote some of the finest country material of his day; songs that were uniquely geared to his own vocal range and style. It also didn't hurt that Phillips' use of tape delay or 'slapback' echo was nowhere better suited than on Cash's records. His stark baritone became even more lonesome sounding when fed through Sun echo. The 'chigga-ching chigga-ching' rhythm that Cash made famous (and vice versa) became even more sticky and impenetrable when fed through slapback echo ... Phillips also had Cash insert a piece of paper between the strings on the neck of his guitar. When Cash strummed it simulated the sound produced by brushes on a snare drum. Finally, to his credit, Phillips never considered fleshing out Cash's sound with fiddle or steel guitar. As he later mused, 'Can you hear "I Walk the Line" with a steel guitar added to it?'"[4]

It's a misnomer, really, to call Cash's early sound "rockabilly," or to place him, Perkins, and Grant in that camp—their approach never quite fit the rockabilly mold. Cash's almost mournful voice and his band's stark, simple—and often repetitive—structures and melodies were never amped up enough to chase down the splash of rockabilly's hip-shaking grooves.

Despite the trio's ill-fitting pop demeanor, "Hey, Porter!"—Cash's very first single for Sun—was a hit, selling more than 100,000 copies (and growing) regionally. A few months later, Cash received his first royalty check from Sun—a whopping $2.41.

To add insult to injury, now that he had a record out, Cash owed fifteen dollars in dues to the American Federation of Musicians. His brother Roy's wife, Wandene, offered to let Cash borrow the money. But he was too excited to be put off by what would be a very temporary shortage of funds: "It wasn't the money I was making from the records as much as the fact that they were hitting," he insisted.[5]

## HITTING THE ROAD

*"I've lived out here so long and know it all so well that I can wake up anywhere in the United States, glance out the bus window, and pinpoint my position to within five miles ... Like the song says, 'I've been everywhere, man. Twice."* [6]
—Johnny Cash

What it meant in the 1950s to "go on tour" meant something altogether different than it does in the new millennium. Besides the obvious points of departure (i.e., present day: better equipment, better transportation, better accommodations, loads more money, etc.), pop artists in the 1950s were expected to pretty much stay on the road indefinitely—or at least till their fame dried up. The road was their bread and butter—the one constant source of income in between the royalty checks that appeared in their mailboxes a few times a year.

Fortunately for Cash, the rootless existence of the road has always suited his complicated, loner personality. "I love the road," he said. "I love being a gypsy. In some important ways I live for it, and in other ways it keeps me alive. If I couldn't keep traveling the world and singing my songs to real, live people who want to hear them, I think I might just sit myself down in front of a TV and start to die."[7]

Another advantage to constant touring was that it turned Cash and his band into pros very quickly. It took working under less-than-desirable conditions—with a different obstacle to overcome seemingly each night—before Cash learned how to seize and hold an audience that hadn't a clue who he was and couldn't have cared less.[8]

But unfortunately, Vivian waned fairly quickly to the prospect of Cash being away for long periods. Despite her early support for Cash's musical ambitions, what he was embarking on wasn't what she had in mind when she exchanged vows with him.

"The first big problem between us began on August 5, 1955, the night I played the first big concert of my career, at the Overton Park Band Shell, with Elvis headlining," Cash said. "The show went well, and Elvis asked me to go on tour with him. I accepted, and took Vivian along, as usual, and it scared her. Once she saw how women went nuts over Elvis and realized that I was heading into that world, she cooled considerably on the whole idea of my recording and touring career."[9]

By the time the Cashes' second daughter (Kathleen) was born, Johnny was barely at home. He later acknowledged the damage it did—and that nothing he could do would give him a second chance at the missed school plays, Fourth of July picnics, and other mundane but still significant events in the lives of his children—not to mention how it debilitated his relationship with Vivian.

It's important to note, however, that Cash didn't swallow the exotic bait of roadwork completely—it's apparent that he struggled with a decision that he couldn't easily undo. This manifested itself early in Cash's career, when he took in a show by a versatile performer of the day, Sonny James—also a Christian. After James' show, Cash got together with him and picked his brain for advice.

"'Sonny,' I said, 'I know you're a Christian, and so am I. I know I was meant to be in the music and entertainment world, but how do you live a Christian life in this business?' Sonny thought for a minute. 'John,' he said, 'the way I do it is by being what I am. I am not just an entertainer who became a Christian. I am a Christian who chose to be an entertainer. I am first a Christian.'"[10]

## CARL, ROY, AND JERRY LEE

For better or worse, Cash wasn't left all alone on the road. Besides the consistent presence of the Tennessee Two, the likes of Carl Perkins (no relation to Luther), Roy Orbison, and a newcomer fireball named Jerry Lee Lewis—all label mates of Cash—regularly hit the concert trail with him on exhausting package tours.

Lewis, unsurprisingly, was completely off his head, even then. That was further complicated by fact that he had just left Bible school before joining Sun, so Lewis did a little preaching to Cash, Perkins, and Orbison.

Oddly, while Lewis cast fire and brimstone at the other three for, in his mind, leading their audiences to sin, Lewis reserved as much heat for himself, freely admitting that he was doing the same thing every time he performed songs like "Whole Lot of Shakin' Going On."[11]

"I will never forget going on tour the first time with him in a car … He started in preaching to us, telling us we were all going to hell. And I said, 'Well, what about you?' And he said, 'Well, I'm going to hell, too. We're all out here doing the devil's work.' I said, 'I'm not doing the devil's work. I'm doing it by the grace of God because it's what I want to do.'"[12]

Carl Perkins—who was raised with fundamental Christian values, just as Cash was—also saw things in a completely different light, which made for some fiery discussions with Lewis. Cash often tried his hand at mediation, as well: "Maybe we just ought to sing whatever we sing, if they like it, and get their attention that way. Then sing them gospel" (not unlike his M.O. following his rededication to Christ in the early 1970s).

"I believe Jerry Lee still sees it as a red-hot issue," Cash noted. "And he may be right."[13]

"Neither [Carl nor I were] walking the line as Christians, but both of us clung to our beliefs," Cash remembered. "Carl had great faith, and at his depths, when he was drunkest, what he'd talk about was God and guilt—the same subjects I would bring up when I was in my worst shape."[14]

## SETTING SUN

Right on the heels of "Hey, Porter!" the Cash hit-making machine rambled on with "Folsom Prison Blues." But his next offering for Phillips turned Cash into a nationwide star.

Written for Vivian as a pledge of fidelity in the face of a temptation-laced life on the road, "I Walk the Line" was the first bona-fide country hit (it reached number two in the C&W charts) to cross over to the pop charts, where it reached number 17 and sold 2 million copies. With "I Walk the Line," Cash became a marketable force in the big cities and college campuses—it was even the title track for the 1970 film starring Gregory Peck—and his career was forever changed.

Cash also was keen to avoid repeating himself too much, so Cowboy Jack Clement was brought in to gussy up Cash's austere visage. It worked like a charm. "Ballad of a Teenage Queen" (C&W #1; pop #14) was augmented with a soprano and chorus, a total departure vocally for Cash, but one that got listeners' collective attention.

But in the midst of his growing success, Cash was dissatisfied with Phillips and Sun in 1958. While part of his discontent stemmed from Cash's desire to make more money on a larger label, a major sticking point was Phillips' continued refusal to release Cash's gospel music.

Again, Phillips didn't want to take the risk of interrupting the string of hits he had with Cash (and other artists) by allowing such an artistic about-face. In retrospect, however, Cash's career would've easily survived a few bumps in the road even if his sacred music fell flat in the charts.

Don Law, a producer from Columbia Records, called Cash to see if he'd be interested in a new recording contract when his Sun deal expired. Cash was more than willing to talk—and was especially pleased that Law was keen on releasing his gospel material. So, the restless Cash rambled once again—unbeknownst to Phillips, who asked Cash point blank if he'd signed a contract option elsewhere. Cash denied it—and to this day doesn't know why he lied to Phillips. And when the truth came out, the Sun Records founder was furious. Cash, now a lame duck at Sun, was still contractually obligated to record a certain number of singles, which he did (among them one of his biggest hits on the label, "Guess Things Happen That Way"—C&W #1; pop #11).

In the meantime, Cash was busy putting together material that would make up 1959's *Hymns by Johnny Cash*, the gospel album Phillips wouldn't let him make. He also continued writing hit songs for Columbia, among them "Don't Take Your Guns to Town," "I Got Stripes," and "Five Feet High and Risin'." And about that time drummer W.S. Holland joined the fray, turning the Tennessee Two into the Tennessee Three.

And while Cash had been a far cry from hustling pay via used washing machine sales anymore, his new contract with Columbia was indeed a better deal than his contract with Sun. The more Cash recorded, the more money he made; the more shows he played, the more money he made. The financial windfall was as addictive as the constant travel. A ten-day tour through Canada and the Midwest grossed him $70,000. Cash's shows sold out weeks in advance. In the year 1959, Cash earned a quarter of a million dollars.

## IS JOHNNY CHANGING?

Here's how *Time* magazine described the new Cash lifestyle following his move with Vivian and the kids to Johnny Carson's old house in Encino, California: "By Hollywood standards, Johnny Cash's $50,000 ranch house, the single Cadillac, and the li'l old Ford Thunderbird are unspectacular. But by anybody's standards the Cash household is unhinged. Around the swimming pool, by day, a trio of little girls raise continual riot. A yellow parrot named Jethroe screeches, whistles and squawks, 'There's a girl' whenever Momma glides past in skin-tight velvet pants. A hefty brother-in-law lounges around listening to a recording of rock 'n' roll music that he composes himself. Through it all, Johnny Cash, head of the household, relaxes in pointy leather loafers, and practices a fast draw with his Colt .45."[15]

By the time 1960 rolled around, Cash finally conceded that

nightclubs were okay to play after all—the money was just too good to pass up. He also appeared in his first movie. In *Five Minutes to Live*, Cash was supposed to kiss the leading lady as she slipped on her nylon stockings, but he refused, arguing such an act—even if it was only acting—was against his moral principles. "Ten years later in his next film, *Gunfight*, he again refused to play a scene with an actress who this time was altogether naked. If movies changed in a decade, Cash's Baptist scruples didn't."[16]

By 1961, Cash estimated that he was giving 290 shows annually over a circuit of 300,000 miles. The audiences averaged at least 3,000 people per performance, which meant he was singing to nearly a million people a year. When he wasn't out performing, he was making more records for Columbia.

There was no letup.

And as the strain compounded, Cash needed something to combat it. Anything to reduce the stress …

CHAPTER SIX

# DEMON PILL POSSESSION

*"You know, I used to sing, 'Were You There When They Crucified My Lord?' while I was stoned on amphetamines. I used to sing all those gospel songs, but I really never felt them. And maybe I was a little bit ashamed of myself at the time because of the hypocrisy of it all: there I was, singing the praises of the Lord and singing about the beauty and the peace you can find in Him—and I was stoned."*[1]

JOHNNY CASH TOOK HIS FIRST AMPHETAMINE tablet—a tiny white Benzedrine pill (scored with a cross of all things)—on the road in 1957.

He loved it.

"It increased my energy, it sharpened my wit, it banished my shyness, it improved my timing, it turned me on like electricity flowing through a light bulb," Cash revealed.

Cash's touring schedule remained insane, and those demon pills pepped up the tired Man in Black and gave him energy to perform in front of an audience.

Before long, Cash was experimenting with dozens of different pills—different names, different colors, different sizes. Dexedrine, Benzedrine, Dexamyl. Of all the colors, the black pills (interestingly enough) were the real barnburners—they'd "take you all the way to California and back in a '53 Cadillac with no sleep."[2]

Amphetamine abuse was only half of Cash's drug problems, however. "Uppers" sped the heartbeat, jolted the system, and could keep exhaustion (and sleep) at bay for unbelievable amounts of time. So in order to combat the uppers' out-of-control side effects, speed freaks need barbiturates (or "downers") in order to calm down, rest, and sleep. The result, obviously, is a constant, debilitating, emotional, and physiological yo-yo that most abusers find almost impossible to give up.

"Every pill I took was an attempt to regain the wonderful, natural feeling of euphoria I experienced the first time," Cash admitted. "Not a single one of them, not even one among the many thousands that slowly tore me away from my family and my God and myself, ever worked. It was never as great as the first time, no matter how hard I tried to make it so."[3]

First, the guilt happened, slapping Cash in the face over nasty things he remembers saying to others or insane, destructive acts he carried out. Sometimes he'd forget to call home and say goodnight to his girls. Sometimes he'd feel so bad about what he did the night before that his only solace was another pill—and, indeed, he'd feel a little better, then better still the more the amphetamine kicked in, until he couldn't wait to repeat the cycle of euphoria. But even as the binges grew out of control, Cash crashed harder and harder when it was over ... and what was the quickest, easiest way to deal? Another pill. Repeat cycle, each time more intense.[4]

"All mood-altering drugs carry a demon called Deception," Cash declared. "You think, 'If this is so bad, why does it feel so good?' I used to tell myself, God created this; it's got to be the greatest thing in the world. But it's like the old saying about the wino: he starts by drinking out of the bottle, and then the bottle starts drinking out of him. The person starts by taking the drugs, but then the drugs start taking the person. That's what happened to me."[5]

For almost the next ten years, Cash gave himself over to pills.

## A CRUMBLING FOUNDATION

Aside from the obvious toll his drug abuse was taking on Cash's body and mind, it was also widening the gulf between him and Vivian—and theirs wasn't the strongest of unions to begin with.

"She saw them as deadly right from the start," Cash remembered. "She urged me not to take them, and of course that just drove the wedge deeper between us. I shrugged her off. Then, as my habit escalated, she actually begged me—'Please, please, get off those pills. They're going to destroy us both!' But I hunched up into myself and let it roll off my back."[6]

So dependent was Cash on uppers and downers that he actually began planning ahead—especially for his tours—coordinating the filling of prescriptions and the locations of his connections. Should he risk not having an abundant supply when he needed them? Or maybe he ought to just drive to that druggist an hour away and get a few hundred pills under the counter, just in case his regular prescription sources didn't pan out?

In addition, Cash found himself abusing other substances—soon he was drinking alcohol (never much of a draw for Cash before he got hooked on pills). The beverages of choice were usually wine or beer—to take the edge off the high if it got too sharp or to knock him out after being up for days.

His abuse progressed to the point where he feared being clean more than he feared dying from an overdose or accident. Still, after Cash's rare drug-free stretches (usually only two or three days at the most), he started feeling pretty good. "Then, though, I'd get home, usually on a Monday, and I'd find the stress of my marriage so hard that I'd drive to that druggist, get two or three hundred pills, head out into the desert in my camper, and stay out there, high, for as long as I could. Sometimes it was days ... my habit just got worse, never better."[7]

Before long Cash's preoccupation with drugs was no longer much of a secret—but any attempts by others to pull him from the chemical morass fell on deaf ears.

There were, however, some voices Cash did heed.

"It was like I was living with a bunch of demons," Cash recounted to one interviewer. "[I drove] into the desert, and I'd start talking to them ... and they'd talk back to me—and I could hear them. I mean, they'd say, 'Go on, John, take twenty more milligrams of Dexedrine, you'll be all right.' And I'd say, 'Yeah, but I've already had forty today.' And they'd answer, 'Take twenty more, it'll be good for you, it'll make you feel just fine.' So I'd take 'em and then continue talking back and forth to the demons inside me."[8]

## RING OF FIRE

The earnest kid who once begged Sam Phillips for a shot at

stardom just a few years before was dead. Or at best, dying. In his place was a ruined man who'd aged twenty years in a fraction of that time, ravaging his mortal coil through substance abuse. Cash's life on every level—professional, personal, and spiritual—was out of control. He was killing himself from the inside out. Everybody knew it, but no one could stop him. Death and destruction lingered at every turn, but Cash didn't slow down. He just sped things up.

Even June Carter's formal entrée into the Cash touring ensemble in December 1961 didn't quell his insanity. If anything, it made life more complicated for Cash and Carter, whose mutual attraction slowly became clear to fans, friends, and family members alike.

Still, Cash managed to increase his popularity more than ever, drawing more and more fans to his shows every year. He recorded "Ring of Fire," written by June Carter and Merle Kilgore, in 1963—it was an unqualified smash.

But it raised a lot of eyebrows in Nashville, for several reasons. The first was due to the Mexican-styled trumpets accenting the melody—and trumpets were a no-no for country tunes. But Cash, beginning to define himself as a rule-breaker in more ways than one, was adamant about including them just as he'd heard them in a dream.[9]

"Ring of Fire" also raised eyebrows because of how openly Carter seemed to be referring to her attraction toward Cash. It wasn't any mystery to Cash, though—he knew the lyrics were about him: *The taste of love is sweet/ When hearts like ours meet/ I fell for you like a child/ Oh, but the fire went wild …* [10]

Some of those words, June recently revealed, are "scary" to her now. "When I fell in love with [Johnny], it was a very painful thing."[11]

"I certainly didn't tell him how I felt," she recalled. "It was not a convenient time for me to fall in love with him—and it wasn't a convenient time for him to fall in love with me. One morning, about four o'clock, I was driving my car just about as fast as I could. I thought, 'Why am I out on the highway this time of night?' I was miserable, and it all came to me: 'I'm falling in love with somebody I have no right to fall in love with.'"[12]

And despite all the crazy distractions and his most heinous responses to them, it was as if Cash thought of himself as immune to harm, even death—it just couldn't nab him. And that just made Cash—full of the dark, frenetic, crazed energy of a very angry man—more determined to see just how far he could take his abuse—the abuse of himself, of his friends, family, and fans, and of his withering soul.

"I was frightened of his way of life," June continued. "I'd watched Hank Williams die. I was part of his life—I'm Hank Jr.'s godmother—and I'd grieved. So I thought, 'I can't fall in love with this man, but it's just like a ring of fire.' I wanted so to play the song for John, but I knew he would see right through me."[13]

In retrospect, Cash believed the fire he experienced with June was, in part, redemptive. Cleansing even. "It made me believe everything was all right, because it felt so good," he said. "When we fell in love, she took it upon herself to be responsible for me staying alive. I didn't think I was killing myself, but you're on the suicide track when you're doing what I was doing. Amphetamines and alcohol will make you crazy, boy!"[14]

During this period, for example, Cash was a frequent visitor to "Jesse," the camper he christened after the outlaw Jesse James. "I was an outlaw, and it had to be one, too," Cash quipped. "I imagined my Jesse to be a free, rebellious spirit, living to ramble in the back of beyond and carry [us] away from people and their needs and their laws. I painted his windows black so I could sleep in him during the daylight, but also because I just liked to spray-paint things black."[15]

But once while escaping life with Jesse in the mountains, Cash started a major forest fire. It was an accident, but his faux pas cost him $125,000 in fines (about $1 million today). Cash is, in fact, the only citizen the U.S. government has ever successfully sued—and collected from—for starting a forest fire.[16]

Yet Cash still found a way to get to church. He happened upon the non-denominational Avenue Community Church in Ventura, California (at this point Cash's home base), one Sunday, and the Reverend Floyd Gressett—a preacher from Comanche, Texas—spotted Cash sitting by himself among the congregation. After several weeks of attendance, the preacher asked Cash if he wanted to join the church. Cash promised that he would come when he was ready.

In February 1963, Gressett got a note from Cash: "Once I told you that I would join your church when the time is right. Now is the time. Since music is my specialty, you can expect me to have songs played when I am here. If nobody wants to hear me sing, that's fine ... Concerning a guitar in church, near the end of the Psalms there is a chapter saying, 'Praise the Lord with all stringed instruments and a loud noise' or something to that effect ... My 'name' doesn't have any bearing. My heart is a pauper like all men. Only I as a 'soldier' will be judged."[17]

## CONTINUING SUCCESS

In the shadow of his addiction, Cash was stronger than ever musically—actually producing a series of concept albums about the working man (*Blood, Sweat and Tears*), cowboys (*Ballads of the True West*), and Native Americans (*Bitter Tears*). On the latter, Cash championed one particular Native American who shined by helping to raise the American flag on Iwo Jima during World War II, only to die a decade later, alone, in a field on the Pima Indian Reservation in Arizona, a down-and-out alcoholic. "The Ballad Of Ira Hayes" ensures he won't be forgotten: *They let him raise the flag and lower it like you would throw a dog a bone/ He died drunk early one morning alone in the land he'd fought to save/ Two inches of water in a lonely ditch was the grave for Ira Hayes …* [18]

## BROKEN THINGS

In the end, while Cash and Gressett became friends, there wasn't anything the preacher could do, either, to help Cash get better—and Cash continued down his destructive path.

He ended up wrecking every car he ever owned in those days. He even "wrecked June's brand new Cadillac. In fact, I managed to get fired from the Grand Ole Opry [after smashing all the footlights with his microphone stand] and total my future wife's car all in the same night."[19]

Seems Cash commandeered June's car and promptly hit a utility pole head-on. He smashed his face into the steering wheel, breaking his nose and forcing his front teeth through his upper lip. Worse yet, the pole snapped and fell on the roof of the Caddy, spreading high-voltage wires on the wet pavement around the car. "It looked like Christmas," Cash recalled, "or hell, take your pick, a warm fiery glow all around … "

Given his state of mind, he miraculously decided against getting out of the car. Besides, there was work to do: namely, stashing beer bottles and pills before Nashville's finest arrived. When they did, Cash was taken to Vanderbilt

Hospital, just a few blocks away.

Before resetting his nose, the doctor attending to Cash was about to give him morphine, and Cash refused the drip—morphine was the last substance he needed inside him. "You won't be able to stand it if I don't," the doctor warned.

"Yeah?" Cash shot back, "Well, go ahead. I want to experience it."

Indeed, Cash could feel bones in his nose scraping and cracking as the doctor reset his nose—and yes, it hurt like the devil.[20]

## JUNE'S SWOON

Despite Cash and Carter's marriages to other people, they nevertheless were acting like an old couple after a while. June told Cash she could help him, that she knew his pain and loneliness, that they were soul mates. So she set out to break down Cash's drug habit.

She searched for his pills and flushed them down the toilet. She prayed for him. She loved him. She stuck to Cash like glue, enduring his antagonism day after day, week after week, month after month.

Despite June's devotion, Cash continued his abuse. "I just went on and on," he recalled. "I was taking amphetamines by the handful, literally, and barbiturates by the handful, too—not to sleep, but just to stop shaking from the amphetamines."

Cash cancelled shows and recording dates. And even when he showed up, his throat was usually too dry to sing because of the pills. His weight was down to 155 pounds (on a six-foot, one-and-a-half-inch frame). He was in and out of jail cells. "I was a waking vision of death," Cash admitted. "And that's exactly how I felt. I was scraping the filthy bottom of the barrel of life."[21]

Worse still, Cash began carrying a gun—a decision he hoped would cure his fears that "everyone was plotting against me." Plus, after a few times in jail, he began thinking that the police were the enemy. "If I saw a police car, I'd duck down a side street, then drive like mad through residential areas, narrowly missing innocent pedestrians," Cash said. "Why I didn't kill anyone, I don't know—or maybe I do know."[22]

## RUNNING FROM GOD?

"I know that the hand of God was never off me, no matter what condition I was in," Cash said later. "For there is no other way to explain my escaping the many, many accidents I had." (In addition to crashing every car he owned for seven straight years, he totaled two jeeps and a camper, turned over two tractors and a bulldozer, sank two boats in separate accidents on a lake, and jumped from a truck just before it went over a 600-hundred-foot cliff in California.)[23]

It's just that Cash was too proud to go to God for help. He later acknowledged that he "held onto that pride of self. To repent and reform all the way to righteousness requires a man to first recognize and admit he has been all wrong ... And I didn't care to admit that."[24]

Yet God apparently wasn't giving up on Cash.

Often following a binge of being awake and wasted for days, Cash would finally rest, and the violent voices inside him quieted down. It was then that he thought "the evil presences left me, [and] there would move in gently about me a warm, sweet presence, and a still, small voice would breathe forth inside my being: 'I am your God. I am still here. I am still waiting. I still love you.'"[25]

It's significant to note the strangely oppositional musical paths Cash took during his down-and-drugged-out period. While most artists' music would tend to reflect their depressed or desperate state, Cash instead managed to consistently release gospel material for Columbia during this time—music that had been at the core of his heart's desire while with Sun in the '50s. After his debut project for Columbia in 1959, *Hymns by Johnny Cash,* a second all-gospel album, *Hymns from the Heart,* was released in 1962. Future projects would regularly feature at least one gospel song as well.

While it can be argued that Cash was expert at compartmentalizing his life in order to keep more plates in the air—even ideological ones—it perhaps makes more sense that his gospel music and attempts at Christian fellowship were ways of "repenting" for his law- and health-defying behavior.

## PAYING THE PRICE

Cash's first arrest occurred in October of 1965. It was late at night, and he was on his way from Juarez, Mexico, crossing the U.S.-Mexico border at El Paso, Texas. During the customs inspection, border patrol found more than 1,000 pills in Cash's possession. They were crammed into a guitar case, and he was arrested and jailed on the spot.

The penalty: a suspended thirty-day sentence and a $1,000 fine. But those slaps on the wrist were the least of Cash's concerns.

Wire-service stories of his arrest and conviction traveled all across America, and reporters relentlessly questioned him, and photographers took his picture as he left the courthouse after paying the fine. And suddenly all the world was reading about Cash's drug problem.[26]

While in jail, Cash told himself he just wanted to stay in his cell alone, pray that God forgives him, and then die, "because I'm too weak to face everyone I'll have to face," he said. "Knowing my family is heartbroken, knowing my friends and fans are hurt and disappointed—it's more than I can reconcile with them."[27]

Meanwhile, Vivian Cash—an innocent bystander in this mess—had received the short end of the stick from her husband for far too long. "Vivian was a wonderful lady," fellow country star George Jones said. "She went through a hell of a lot with him. I know she couldn't stand it anymore."[28]

"He's got a mind of his own," Vivian once told writer Christopher S. Wren. "If he makes up his mind to do something, he's going to do it, come hell or high water. They all make it look like I got him on pills and that woman got him off pills. [But] if there was anything left to do, I did it. I tried everything in the book. Johnny knows to this day that I've never lied to him. I said to him in our bedroom in Casitas Springs, 'Please tell me what I can do to help you.' He said, 'I really appreciate it, but nobody can help me but myself.' I did live in hell without anybody knowing it. I never put him down because he is the girls' father. What's happened has happened, and there's no way to erase it. But as Grandma Cash says, 'Whatever you sow, so shall you reap.'"[29]

## MOMENTS OF TRUTH

Soon June Carter separated from her second husband, Rip Nix. She was so ashamed that for six months she kept it a secret, telling not even her mother, or Marshall Grant, or even

Cash. Worse still, she was more aware than ever that she was falling in love with the drug-addled singer, her touring partner, and her guilt was almost unbearable. "I used to go to church about every day for a year. I used to get out my Bible and look through it. I used to go into the bathroom, and wear out my knees and pray."[30]

Cash followed suit, leaving Vivian in June 1966. By August 1967, Vivian filed for divorce, citing extreme cruelty, and Cash did not contest it. At that point he lost all interest in eating, shrinking down to less than 140 pounds. And more than once his troupe got him dressed, pointed him toward the stage, and watched while he somehow brought the house down, "barely able to stand at the microphone, somehow still generating more musical excitement that anyone in the audience could remember ever feeling before."[31]

A doctor friend, psychiatrist Nat Winston, was convinced the end was near. "You can't believe how tense he was when he was on pills," Winston remembered. "He was haggard, a mess. He was out of control. I don't think he would have lived much longer. He would have died or killed himself in an accident. In some ways, he enjoyed the pathos. He knew he had great talent and was burning himself out."[32]

Cash knew better, though.

"I was running from God and whatever He wanted me to do," he realized later. "But I knew I'd tire before He would, and I'd make the change before He gave up on me. And He never did. So I gave up, reached up, and He pulled me to my feet.[33]

But first, Johnny Cash would have to crawl.

CHAPTER SEVEN

# NICKAJACK CAVE AND THE WAY HOME

BY EARLY OCTOBER 1967, JOHNNY CASH reached the end—the end of himself. Whoever that was.

Weak and defeated after going yet again without sleep or food for several days, the Man in Black looked inside himself and saw nothing but darkness. Cash surmised that entering the next life was his best option of escape. "I never wanted to see another dawn. I had wasted my life. I had drifted so far away from God and every stabilizing force in my life that I felt there was no hope for me."[1]

The answer came to him in a flash: Nickajack Cave. He'd drive to the remote locale on the Tennessee River, just north of Chattanooga, and let God take him from the world and do whatever He wanted after that point—even being welcomed into heaven wasn't a sure thing anymore to Cash.

"I couldn't stand myself anymore," he recalled later. "I wanted to get away from me. And if that meant dyin', then okay, I'm ready."[2]

When Nickajack Cave was open (the Army Corps of Engineers have since put a dam in, which closed off the entrance), it was quite the sight. Its opening was 150 feet wide and 50 feet high and led into a system of caves—some of them larger than two or three football stadiums—all which ran under the mountains all the way down into Alabama. Cash had visited the caves several times before in search of Civil War and Native American artifacts.

Its moniker was born after Andrew Jackson and his army killed the Nickajack Indians there—men, women, and children. The Indians left their bones in mounds, and legend has it that their ghosts haunt the cave. Nickajack was also a refuge for the Confederate soldiers in the battle of Missionary Ridge and Lookout Mountain.[3] During the Civil War, soldiers from both the North and the South escaped the elements in the caves, leaving their names and messages carved into the limestone.

In later years, many spelunkers and amateur adventurers died in Nickajack Cave after getting lost in the pitch-black passageways—and that's exactly what Cash had in mind for himself.

"If I crawled in far enough," he figured, "I'd never be able to find my way back out, and nobody would be able to locate me until I was dead—if indeed they ever could. Plus, the dam would be going in soon."[4]

So Cash parked his Jeep, walked through the cave's entrance, and started crawling. He crawled and crawled and crawled—it must have gone on for two or three hours at least. That's when his flashlight batteries wore out. Finally he could lie down to die in total darkness.

"The absolute lack of light was appropriate," Cash wrote in his autobiography, "for at that moment I was as far from God as I have ever been. My separation from Him, the deepest and ravaging of the various kinds of loneliness I'd felt over the years, seemed finally complete."[5]

But it wasn't.

Cash figured that God would never follow him into this dark, lonely place—especially after all the wrong he'd done and all the pain and hurt he caused over the years. "I thought I'd left Him, but He hadn't left me," Cash explained. "I felt something very powerful start to happen to me, a sensation of utter peace, clarity, and sobriety ... How, after being awake for so long and driving my body so hard and taking so many pills ... could I possibly feel all right?

"The feeling persisted, though, and then my mind started focusing on God ... I became conscious of a very clear, simple idea: I was not in charge of my destiny. I was not in charge of my own death. I was going to die at God's time, not mine. I hadn't prayed over my decision to seek death in the cave, but that hadn't stopped God from intervening."[6]

Those first flickers of light, of hope, were enough to get Cash thinking how he could live through this ordeal. But the first problem was that he was indeed enveloped in total darkness—he hadn't a clue which direction would lead him out of the cave. Quite the obstacle after three hours of travel into the cave—forget the complex maze of passageways and chambers between him and his Jeep.

Despite the daunting task ahead, Cash started to crawl again—and this time, he was crawling in search of the light, not the dark. He did so energetically but calmly, in whatever direction instinct told him to go. He gradually felt ahead with his hands to prevent himself from falling into some ravine. Crablike. Determined.

After an unknown amount of time, Cash finally felt a breeze on his back. He knew then that wherever the breeze was coming from was the way out. Excitedly he followed the wind until he saw light, and then, finally, the cave opening. "I don't know how I got out, 'cept God got me out," Cash said.[7]

Incredibly, June was there with a basket of food and drink, as well as Carrie Cash. He was confused: Wasn't his momma in California? Yes, she had been. "I knew something was wrong," she said. "I had to come and find you."[8]

As June and Carrie drove Cash back toward Nashville, he told his momma that God saved him from killing himself—and that he was ready to commit himself to God and do whatever it took to beat his drug habit.

This time he wasn't fooling himself.

## ON THE WAY HOME

Cash decided that he was going to beat his addiction, and he jumped into the fray with gusto—he needed to, as Cash was in for the fight of his life. He retreated to a house he'd just purchased on Old Hickory Lake and settled in for days and weeks of withdrawal, then (hopefully) recovery. June and her mother and father "formed a circle of faith around me, caring for me and insulating me from the outside world, particularly the people, some of them close friends, who'd been doing drugs with me."[9]

June loved Johnny. She fed him when he was too weak to eat, nursed him back to strength when he was sick, and eventually helped him find the will to turn things around.

Dr. Winston, then Tennessee's commissioner for public health, came to the house every day, holding Cash's feet to the fire and giving him vital support. It was a 10,000-to-1 shot, but some part of Cash responded to the crisis.[10]

"The doctor came to see me every day at 5 p.m." Cash said. "The first few days I was still rollin' stones. Amphetamine was my drug of choice, and I had pills hidden all over this room—I was serious about quitting, but not quite. About the third or fourth day, the doctor looked me in the eye and asked, 'How you doin?'"

"I said, 'Great!'

"And he said, 'Bulls--t. I know you're not doing great. When are you going to get rid of them?' So I went and got them out of the closet and wherever else I had them hid, and we flushed them. Then I really started the program that he laid out for me."[11]

## NIGHTMARES

"I didn't have the peace inside for a lot of praying, but every breath was a prayer, a fighting prayer, and I wasn't giving up," Cash noted. "I had turned it over to God. I had humbled myself. I was asking Him to help."[12]

By the third night, Cash was finally able to fall asleep at about 3 a.m. But what he experienced that night—and every night for the next ten days—was anything but comforting.

The nightmare started in his stomach (probably because that's where the pills did their work), and at first Cash would lie on his back or curled up on his side. Then the cramps came, and he'd roll over, doze off, and go to sleep.

All of a sudden Cash sensed a glass ball expanding in his gut, growing to the size of a baseball, then a volleyball, then a basketball, then twice the size of a basketball—until it lifted Cash off the bed and through the ceiling. He sensed he was somewhere between awake and asleep, but Cash had little control over the disconcerting things he was seeing and feeling in his nightmare.

The glass ball then exploded, sending microscopic shards into his bloodstream, through his heart, into the veins of his arms, legs, feet, neck, and brain. They even seeped through the pores of his skin. He wanted to scream, but he couldn't. Then Cash floated down through the ceiling and onto the bed and woke up. He was relieved that the nightmare was over, but Cash still needed to sleep—and when he finally would fall back asleep, the same nightmare happened (except for the times the shards of glass were replaced with splinters, briers, thorns, and sometimes even worms). That's how it was for a while, until the drugs worked their way out of his system.[13]

After the withdrawal period was over and when he was well

enough to get around, Dr. Winston encouraged Cash to run through the woods for exercise. Indeed, Cash's appetite returned in no time, and he quickly put weight back on, going from 140 to 200 pounds.[14]

"I've never seen anybody come off pills with the guts that he showed," Winston noted incredulously. "He was really fighting. But he was fighting on his terms. A miserably low percentage of people who are hooked can make it. I have a feeling that he's made it."[15]

Cash agreed. "Most everybody had written me off. Oh yeah, they all acted like they were proud for me when I straightened up. Some of them are still mad about it, though. I didn't go ahead and die so they'd have a legend to sing about and put me in hillbilly heaven!"[16]

But most of all, Cash was thankful to God that he was finally getting over his life-threatening addiction—and he recognized that Christ's strength was what pulled him through.

"I undressed and got on my knees beside the bed, but the words wouldn't come," he remembered. "I couldn't put into human language all the things for which I wanted to thank Him: for the peace I was feeling now; for the years He has pulled me through; for the bright future; for life itself. I stayed that way for a long, long time, kneeling with my head in my hands, my mind racing back over the years touching on every wrong I could remember doing, clearing my conscience of it.

"The present came into focus. The words still wouldn't come. But my mind was thanking Him for a million blessings that I couldn't see I deserved for any reason.

"My mind also probed the future, and I put it in His hands—told Him by wordless thoughts that I'd do whatever He showed me I should do.

"'Only don't give up on me,' I prayed silently. 'I can't make it without You.'[17]

"God had done more than speak to me. He had revealed His will to me through other people, family, and friends," Cash discovered. "The greatest joy of my life was that I no longer felt separated from Him. Now He is my Counselor, my Rock of Ages to stand upon."[18]

But that didn't necessarily mean Cash was ready to get back to church on a regular basis. Still June prodded him to attend services at the First Baptist Church of Hendersonville with her—even if that meant arriving late and sitting in the back pew. So they did just that.[19]

## SOBER & ONSTAGE

Cash was rebuilding his strength and reconnecting with God. And by November 11, 1967, he was able to face an audience again—a small crowd at the high school in Hendersonville, near his new home. It would be the first time Cash performed sober in more than a decade.

He hit the stage with the biggest case of butterflies and jitters that he'd ever felt, but he prayed and June prayed. After a few songs, Cash felt strong and confident—and thankful. June was crying as she watched Cash becoming a brand-new man—essentially a man she never knew before, as June grew close to Cash when he was already messed up by drug abuse.

Fittingly, he closed the show with "Were You There When They Crucified My Lord?" a song Cash admitted he'd performed high on amphetamines countless times before. But on this night, Cash sang the old spiritual with a clear head and heart—one that was growing closer and closer to the subject of the song.

"I felt about six feet off the floor," Cash revealed. "I felt Him with me. I was more alive than I'd ever been before. I knew I was again holding onto the Man I was singing about in that song, and I knew He was still holding me."[20]

CHAPTER EIGHT

# BEHOLD, ALL THINGS BECOME NEW

"WHAT I REALLY ENJOY IS THE Bible," Cash declared. "I love to set myself a test, give myself something to study. I find a passage I don't quite understand and chase it down in the concordance and the chain references until I learn what it means, or at least what the best-versed scholars have been able to interpret it as meaning."[1]

Not surprisingly, the time following his recovery from drugs was the most intense period devoted to Bible study in Cash's life to that point. He received daily encouragement from June and her parents—Ma and Pop Carter—which immediately led to Cash's voracious devotion to and the study of Scripture.

"I feel that the studies are necessary for experiencing the spiritual growth I need so badly," Cash explained. "I have learned that once you stand up on God's side, the words of wisdom He imparts through the Bible are the weapons you need every day, whether you're a preacher or a guitar picker.[2]

"Pop Carter was the one who really got me going on Bible study," Cash added. "I liked him a great deal, and learned a great deal from him in the days after I came out of Nickajack Cave."[3]

June's daddy was a self-taught theologian and quite the Bible scholar, Cash remembered, and was also a skilled teacher and partner in spiritual discussions—which Cash jumped into with enthusiasm. He was hungry for truth, and Carter imparted all he could to his future son-in-law. That time with Pop Carter led to Johnny and June enrolling in biblical correspondence courses over a three-year period. "We worked on our assignments at home, on the road, on the bus, on planes, and sometimes in a quiet spot like a cabin in the woods near home," Cash noted. "Whenever we had a few minutes or a few hours, we would work on our lessons; then we'd mail them in and await the next course.[4]

"For me the experience was both exciting and humbling," Cash revealed. "I learned just enough to understand that I knew almost nothing."[5]

Many of the books that found their way to the spirituality section of Cash's home library belonged to Pop Carter—gifts that Cash has poured into way more than once: *The Life of Christ* by Fleetwood, *The Life of Christ* by Farrar, *The Life and Acts of Paul the Apostle* by Conebere and Howsom, as well as Bible commentaries, books on the Holy Land, Jewish customs, the Roman Empire, and the lives of the early Christians.

"I've often found strength in the faith and courage of some of those early Church fathers who kept the Word alive for us and refused to reject the Gospel in the face of torture and execution," Cash said.[6]

## AT FOLSOM PRISON

Cash was indeed a new man. A new creation, in many ways. His relationship with God was restored and strengthened. He was finally off pills and performing sober for the first time in a decade. And he was a new man to June as well. She was seeing the Johnny Cash she always sensed was there, but never saw before. And she liked what she saw.

Cash was also embarking on what would become a long period flush with major creative successes—and his new triumphs and emphases would be primarily outside of his comfortable realm of singing to a tape machine or a live audience. Believe it or not, Cash would go on to blaze trails in television and film while his recording and touring career gradually took a back seat. And still, Cash's popularity and appeal as a recording artist and live act nevertheless exploded into the stratosphere in the coming years in ways he never expected.

His first major idea, as a matter of fact, was purely musical—and it came right on the heels of his "comeback" show in Hendersonville:

A concert for the inmates at Folsom Prison in California.

Such an idea wasn't anything radical for Cash—he'd been performing for cons since his song "Folsom Prison Blues" reached the inmates at Huntsville, Texas, in 1957.[7] But this time he'd be playing to a distinctly different audience than the hometown crowd that warmly greeted him after his recovery from drugs.

Cash was resolute, though.

He called on the Rev. Gressett from the Ventura church—the

one to whom he pledged allegiance in the early '60s during his lengthy pill-popping phase. Gressett traveled to Folsom once a month to preach and knew the officials there. Soon the Cash concert behind the Folsom walls was slated for January 13, 1968.

"I was about as relaxed as a bug in a roach motel, being still new to the business of getting up on stage in front of people without a bloodstream full of drugs," Cash admitted. "But once we got into it, that was one good show."[8]

As for his reasons for performing at Folsom Prison, Cash freely admitted the kinship he feels with outlaws and outcasts—those who break the law and have problems with authority. And Cash, who's spent some time in the slammer as well, could have been just a handful of drug busts from Folsom himself had he not cleaned up.

"I have been behind bars a few times—sometimes of my own volition, sometimes involuntarily," Cash said. "I know how lonely they feel, how lonely they are."[9]

As one critic noted, "Cash is big, more than 6 feet, more than 200 pounds, with a mean, pocked-scarred face, unused to smiling. Maybe he likes prison concerts because the convicts react boisterously. Maybe there's a violence bottled up inside him that needs the kinship of violent men. But even when his songs are deadly sad, there's a lilt down deep nothing can hide. It says, 'I'm not poor anymore.' Or, 'There but for the grace of God … '"[10]

But it was his revived appreciation for the parables and teachings of Jesus, specifically Matthew 25:36—"I was in prison, and you came to visit me"—that likely fueled Cash's desire to sing for prisoners.

"I'm just trying to be a good Christian," he emphasized to one interviewer curious about his reasons for reaching out to inmates. "You know, there's three different types of Christians. There's preaching Christians, church-playing Christians, and there's practicing Christians—and I'm trying very hard to be a practicing Christian. If you take the words of Jesus literally and apply them to your everyday life, you discover that the greatest fulfillment you'll ever find really does lie in giving. And that's why I do things like prison concerts."[11]

(During a later concert at the Nevada State Penitentiary, Cash repeated his intentions to the inmates: "We're here because the inmate population petitioned us to come," Cash said. "We're here because we love the applause you give us ... and I'm here because I'm a Christian." No doubt Cash was buoyed by a letter from an inmate after that show, which read, in part: "Dear Johnny, I know now what Jesus meant when He said He was sent to the captives, because I saw Him in you today.")[12]

Listening to the strains of Cash (and later in the show, Carter) singing and interacting with his captive audience on the remastered *At Folsom Prison* album is an ear-opener: The vibe is remarkably fresh and spirited. The snippets of prison officials' announcements from the stage P.A. surely add realism, but the juice is in the enthusiastic hollers and cheers from inmates that punctuate Cash's gritty lyrics—the set is dominated by outlaw- and prison-themed tunes—as well as intense instrumental passages. (A taste of the Cash-Carter barnburning, Grammy-winning duet, "Jackson," with June's gravel-throated vocals besting Cash verse for verse, is a real treat.) In short, the cons love him. He's one of them. Part of the family. Close to the earth. Familiar with struggle. A truth teller. And Johnny loves the cons, too.

*At Folsom Prison* was released later in 1968, hit the top of the *Billboard* charts, and lit even more flames under Cash's already rejuvenated career. Critic Chet Flippo called it the best live album ever—and similar reviews reflected the enthusiasm of the record-buying public.

"With a face that might have been ripped off a wanted poster, a voice that sounds as though it's coming through a bandana mask, songs that may as well be fired from six-guns, and a Bible under his writing arm, Johnny Cash has gone thundering through his career like a night-riding missionary, rousing the country music underground," noted a *Life* magazine reviewer. "As long ago as 1956, with his first pop hit record, 'I Walk the Line,' he pioneered in the lyrical weirdness that is becoming America's new eloquence, a language that speaks to everybody and not just farm hands. He has also been called country music's first psychedelic poet. 'I won't exactly buy that,' he says like a hip John Wayne, 'but I'll accept it.'"[13]

*Time* saw the album as yet another advance by Cash through musical barriers. "It has sold far beyond the usual boundaries of the country market. This is not entirely new for Cash. In his dozen years as a top recording performer, he has broken out of the country category with nationwide pop hits several times before ('I Walk the Line,' 'Ring of Fire'). But the *Folsom* album seems to appeal to a wider, more diverse audience than anything else he has ever done … In fact, the album stands as a timely symbol of the growing infusion of country sounds into the U.S. pop mainstream."[14]

## AT SAN QUENTIN

Cash followed up the groundbreaking success of *At Folsom Prison* with another live album behind bars, *At San Quentin*.

Also a blockbuster, it featured what would become Cash's biggest selling song ever, "A Boy Named Sue," about a kid whose father names him "Sue" so he'll be tough all his life.

The story is that the night before Cash flew to California to play the San Quentin show, June and Johnny threw a party at their house. It was quite the guest list—Bob Dylan, Joni Mitchell, Kris Kristofferson, Graham Nash, and Shel Silverstein, among others. The latter luminaries were sort of expected to "sing for their supper," however, and quite a few debut renditions of legendary songs were aired out: Dylan's "Lay Lady Lay," Mitchell's "Both Sides Now," Kristofferson's "Me and Bobby McGee," Nash's "Marrakesh Express," and Shel Silverstein's "A Boy Named Sue."

The next day June suggested taking the words to "A Boy Named Sue" to California to record during the San Quentin concert. "I don't have time to learn that song before the show," Cash said. But June insisted, so Cash complied. Being really unfamiliar with the new lyrics, Cash placed the lyric sheet on a music stand during the show, and "when it came time that I thought I was brave enough, I did that song."[15]

Cash and his band improvised the melody onstage while Cash sang-read the lyrics by Shel Silverstein. The convicts went wild as Cash barked out the defiant, signature lyric, *My name is Sue! How do you do? Now you gonna die!*[16]

The whole vibe of the raucous event was unnerving—especially for one crucial element at San Quentin.

"The guards were scared to death," he noted later. "All the convicts were standing up on the dining tables. They were out of control, really. During the second rendition of ['San Quentin'] all I would have had to do was say 'Break!' and they were gone, man. They were ready! I've got a book called *Extraordinary Popular Delusions and the Madness of Crowds* that I've studied for years. I knew I had that prison audience where all I had to do was say, 'Take over! Break!' and they would have. Those guards knew it, too. I was tempted. But I thought about June and the Carter Family—they were there with me, too—and I controlled myself. 'Cause I was really ready for some excitement."[17]

## WAS JESUS AN OUTLAW, TOO?

Cash is the best example—maybe the only example—of an artist who sings about love, sings about God, and sings about murder and convicts and jailhouse life ... and means every word he utters. It's due to, again, his vast interior landscape that accommodated many perspectives and emotions and conveyed them to those of us who can't.

As a Christian, Cash had already made his case for why he bothered playing prison yards and cafeterias when he could add another Madison Square Garden engagement to his tour itinerary—not to mention seven more figures to his bank account.

But a less obvious motivation in that regard is found in Cash's liner notes for the *Murder* portion of the *Love God Murder* boxed set, in which he cautiously compared Christ's crucifixion to a murder: "It had all the trappings of a lynching, what with the common populace screaming, 'Crucify Him!' the Sanhedrin, the ruling religious body, saying, 'It is expedient that one man should die for the people.' And, the final authority, the Roman puppet government allowing it to happen by 'washing their hands' of the matter."

Does Cash consider Jesus an outlaw? You'd be hard pressed to say no.

Jesus, after all, has a big-time rap sheet, a police record if you will—and He was arrested and executed. Quite scandalous! If Jesus walked through church doors with such a trail of questionable repute dragging behind Him, would Christians make room for Him in the pews? (Well, maybe after some counseling, a shave, a haircut, and a bath ... )

For Cash, there's probably a little bit of Jesus in Joe Bean, the subject of his *At Folsom Prison* tune of the same name about a twenty-year-old Arkansas kid who died by the hangman's noose for a crime he didn't commit. In this light, perhaps when Cash sings about shooting a man in Reno "just to watch him die," it's a far cry from an endorsement; rather, it's a way of embodying the sad skin of the outlaw, of understanding and zeroing in on a palpable sense of the criminal's pain.

That's, after all, what Jesus did.

## "WE GOT MARRIED IN A FEVER ... "

A month after the Folsom Prison concert was recorded, Cash and Carter were together onstage in London, Ontario, and he picked that moment to propose. The surprised and embarrassed Carter—after some tongue-in-cheek audience coaxing—accepted. With both their divorces final, Cash and Carter were free to do what they probably always wished they could do since they met—and the two exchanged marriage vows on March 1, 1968. Their union lasted thirty-five years until June's death in May 2003.

"We stuck together like glue," Cash said of his new life with

June, who now called herself June Carter Cash. "I gathered strength and gained a little spiritual growth from Bible study and long discussions with June about the Bible, and mainly about Jesus and His teachings."[18]

"They had a deep, really mystical bond—their love for one another," writer Charles Hirshberg said. "It was deeply undergirded by both religion and a total sense, a real deep-down-where-it-counts belief that God had brought them together. They considered their marriage—the fact that they had found each other—to be a miracle of their faith. Their marriage was an absolute religious experience for both of them."[19]

As the years went on, Cash learned exactly how formidable a partner June really was. "She's brilliant. She's got a great personality. She's easy to live with, because she makes it a point to be so. She's loving. She's sharing. The main thing, though, is that she loves me and I know it ... she's my solid rock. She's my spark plug.[20]

But they rarely took themselves too seriously. During one joint interview, June said, "We've shared it all together—the good, the bad, and ..." before she could finish, Johnny deadpanned, "the gnarly."[21]

"There's unconditional love there. You hear that phrase a lot, but it's real with me and her. She loves me in spite of everything, in spite of myself. She has saved my life more than once. She's always been there with her love, and it has certainly made me forget the pain for a long time, many times. When it gets dark, and everybody's gone home and the lights are turned off, it's just me and her."[22]

CHAPTER NINE

# THE JOHNNY CASH SHOW

WITH CASH'S NAME IN THE NATIONAL spotlight once again, ABC—desiring to piggyback on the success of another country music variety show hosted by Glenn Campbell—asked Cash if he'd be into hosting his own show, coast-to-coast. Some music. Some comedy. Some variety.

He was definitely game.

Aside from the massive exposure the weekly, hour-long show would afford him, Cash also saw it as an opportunity to break down some more barriers—both artistically and spiritually.

*The Johnny Cash Show* indeed was groundbreaking—ostensibly a country-oriented show, it nevertheless featured pop-oriented musical guests such as Bob Dylan, Joni Mitchell, Neil Young, Derek and the Dominoes (Eric Clapton's "Layla" group), Linda Ronstadt, Gordon Lightfoot, Jose Feliciano, Neil

Diamond, Ray Charles, Arlo Guthrie, Cass Elliot, Stevie Wonder, James Taylor, and still others. It was a first.

Actually Cash accomplished several things at once: 1) By including pop artists on *The Johnny Cash Show,* he once again bucked the Nashvillian code of "keepin' it country"—demonstrating that he did things his way; 2) He exposed America to many artists who never before had such a far-reaching platform; 3) He still flew the country flag high in the midst of genre diversity, thereby retaining his core audience.

As one critic put it, "More than any other broadcast before it, and maybe since, *The Johnny Cash Show* made hillbilly culture 'cool' with mainstream and even countercultural audiences."[1]

## BOB DYLAN

The most famous musical guest on *The Johnny Cash Show* was undoubtedly Bob Dylan. During the program's very first installment, broadcast on June 7, 1969, the usually reclusive artist played three songs, and his duet with Cash on "Girl from the North Country" made the cut for the nationwide segment. Certainly Dylan wasn't the type to appear on any network program, but Cash had proven a friend and ally over the years, so *The Johnny Cash Show* was a safe place for him.

Cash and Dylan met at the 1964 Newport Folk Festival after a long period of correspondence filled with mutual admiration. "I don't have many memories of the event," Cash noted regarding Newport, "but I do remember June and me and Bob and Joan Baez in my hotel room, so happy to meet each other that we were jumping on the bed like kids."[2]

Dylan began their letter writing years before, telling Cash how much he gained from his early songs, and Cash admitted he was a Dylan fan. Later Cash would lend vocal support to Dylan's *Nashville Skyline* album—and recently noted that *The Freewheelin' Bob Dylan* is still one of his all-time favorite recordings.

Though neither Cash nor Dylan discussed the issue publicly, one wonders to what extent Cash's renewed sense of spirituality throughout the '70s influenced Dylan before (and after) his own conversion to Christianity in 1979 ...

## DIFFICULTIES

While Cash's innovative approach to his show was scoring ratings points, he didn't always get his way with respect to guests. "I want them to call me and tell me why Pete Seeger can't be on my show," Cash sternly told director Bill Carruthers in a Nashville hotel room ... [No] nod came for Seeger, whose banjo and voice had damned the Vietnam war. "I think Pete Seeger is a good American—as good an American as I've ever met."

In addition, there were Cash watchers who felt the show featured too many guests, too much variety, too much slapstick comedy—all blurring the image of the star and leaving the production without definition.[3]

Cash, as usual, was undeterred.

## CONFESSION

The show's inclusion of gospel songs, while a natural for Cash to perform, wasn't necessarily the fare that network television audiences were used to—and as the program gained more and more popularity with an unusually large cross-section of America, a lot of folks started sending letters to Cash, inquiring where Johnny stood on spiritual matters.

On November 18, 1970, Cash gave 'em the skinny:

"Well, folks, I've introduced lots of hymns and gospel songs on this show. I just want to make it clear that I'm feeling what I'm singing about in this next one. I am a Christian … The number-one power in this world is God. The number-two power is Satan, and though he manages to fight for second in my life, I want to dedicate this song to the proposition that God is the victor in my life. I'd be nothing without Him. I want to get in a good lick right now for Number One."[4] With that, Cash performed "I Saw a Man," an Arthur Smith tune from 1956: *He said if I be lifted up, I'll draw all men to me/ He turned and then I saw the nail-scarred hands that bled for me …* [5]

Cash knew he inhabited dangerous ground by publicly declaring his faith in Christ before a national audience. If the scrutiny from the press and backlash from the public wouldn't prove enough to handle, the brass at ABC didn't like his mini-sermon either.

"Well, then," Cash shot back, "you're producing the wrong man here, because gospel music … is part of who I am and part of what I do. I don't cram anything down people's throats, but neither do I make any apologies for it, and in a song introduction, I have to tell it like it is. I'm not going to proselytize, but I'm not going to crawfish, and I'm not going to compromise. So don't you worry about me mentioning Jesus, or God, or Moses, or whomever I decide to mention in the spiritual realm. If you don't like it, you can always edit it."[6]

Cash also knew his confession might have turned off those who took his words as proselytizing—but he felt he needed to go for broke, whatever the consequences, financial or otherwise. "If you want to be a good Christian," he declared, "you have to be willing to give up worldly things in order to stay true to your faith."[7]

*The Johnny Cash Show* ran its course by the spring of 1971—and Cash & Co. went out with a bang, billing the final hour as a gospel music special. Cash brought in the Blackwood Brothers, Mahalia Jackson, Stuart Hamblin, and even Billy Graham. "The whole show was a closing hymn," Cash realized.[8]

## THE FORERUNNER OF CHRISTIAN MUSIC

It must be argued here that the Johnny Cash of the late '60s and early '70s was the forerunner of what today is called contemporary Christian music. Sure, there were Christians on the pop scene already (Pat Boone comes to mind, along with legions of other milquetoasty suspects), but Cash embodied a strong, honest, even a little dangerous, persona that was refreshing and appealing—and that made his rubber-meets-the-road Christianity believable and easy to swallow. Cash's faith in Jesus was pockmarked, imperfect, and still rich with grace, forgiveness, and humility—a faith that many saw as attractive and authentic.

And Cash laid it all on the line for an hour every week on national television—what Christian artist before or since could claim that massive a platform? What's more, Cash's whole shootin' match was completely unaffected by the Christian music industry—because there was no industry to affect Cash or anybody else. (Tellingly, fledgling Christian labels were hatched on the heels of Cash's visible, vocal impact on post flower-power culture, as well as acts that would in later years be canonized as Christian music pioneers.)

It's unlikely that even the legendary Larry Norman—lauded as the "poet laureate" for the Jesus Movement with his 1969 album *Upon This Rock*—took no inspiration from the Man in Black's straightforward, stalwart approach on *The Johnny Cash Show*. And Cash never cloistered himself or limited his contact with "the world"—he played Billy Graham Crusades and the Las Vegas Strip ... and shared his faith in both places.

Johnny Cash had no blueprint for contemporary Christian music—he may have even preferred that it didn't exist—but he was there at the foundation nonetheless.

## "JOHNNY CASH IS COOL"

That's what one hippie teenager said just prior to the start of a Cash concert in 1969.[9] For him, Cash wasn't about country music—which hippie youth pretty much universally despised—Cash was about truth and freedom and fighting the good fight. And if the hippie mantra was to not trust anyone over the age of thirty, Cash was the lone exception to the rule in the late '60s and early '70s. The counterculture liked Cash because of his "affection for the rural poor and the incarcerated, because his profanity-studded language and strange attire place him outside the establishment ... "[10]

In the midst of his chart-topping albums and high-flying TV show that reached a larger audience in one hour than he could ever have reached on the road, Cash hit new levels of popularity as he bulldozed through concert after concert, leaving listeners in Beatle-like hysterics, taking on the persona of a dark-horse pied piper for everyman.

Here's how one critic described the waves of humanity waiting to see Cash during one of those concerts: "American Gothics in bib overalls and dirty-footed hippies are jammed in together, along with mechanics, cab drivers, factory girls, red-faced tractor hands, students ... and a smattering of fashionable suburban types. There are innocent-eyed, gospel-singing folk from the back country and husky T-shirted fellows who are well fortified with beer. And there are even a few of the locality's Amish, with their beards and flat-brimmed hats. This is Republican country, but a town leader avowed that President Nixon wouldn't have drawn such a crowd ... on a hot summer afternoon."[11]

After a comeback show at Carnegie Hall in 1968, a critic noted the capacity crowd that greeted Cash consisted of country music fans and "hipsters and pop musicians rediscovering an old path beneath the faddism of pop music."[12]

But his growing legion of fans were seeing something deeper beyond his simple tunes about love, God, and murder: "He's into hymns, but they aren't excuses to knock the Supreme Court and big-city sin," one writer observed. "When Johnny Cash sings a hymn, you get this very solitary search for grace.

And it's that same quality of struggle resolved, or deferred, or verging on agony that transforms just about everything he sings into what you feel when you're alone in a new room. That's the kind of aloneness the Beatles never touch. It's something Bob Dylan is reaching for now, in the guise of simplicity. To Johnny Cash, it's right out there, like a ... scar."[13]

In other words—Johnny Cash is cool.

CHAPTER TEN

# ALTAR CALL

WHILE THE BLESSINGS IN CASH'S LIFE had been numerous over the previous two years—the restoration of his health, getting on track with God, his marriage to June, two big-selling, critically acclaimed albums (*Folsom* and *San Quentin*), and a smash-hit TV show that Cash filled with more and more gospel music each week and finally used as an understated platform for his faith—there had been hard moments, too.

The most difficult occurred on August 5, 1968, just when things were starting to cook again for Cash & the Tennessee Three.

Luther Perkins fell asleep on his couch with a lit cigarette and died from the burns he received.

The loss of his longtime friend and distinctive guitarist stunned Cash greatly. The loss also opened the door for Larry and Dottie Lee—old Opry friends of Cash and Perkins—to share more of God's love with Johnny. "When [Luther] died it took us out to Johnny and June's house three or four nights in a row, and we got real close," Dottie recalled.[1]

And it was during this time that God was vying for the attention of Joanne Yates, Cash's younger sister, who lived in Nashville and worked at House of Cash, Johnny's merchandise arm to the public. "I was always the black sheep of the family," Yates recalled, "and at this particular time I was really at a crossroads in my personal life. I was ready to make a break in one direction or another ... " And during a very scary plane ride, Yates finally figured it was time to tell God she was going to straighten her life out.[2]

Dottie Lee also saw this as a chance to witness to Yates, so she invited her to Evangel Temple, a small Assembly of God congregation in town pastored by Jimmy R. Snow, son of the country music star, Hank Snow. Evangel was launched as an outreach to music industry types.

What Cash's younger sister remembered best about her first visit to Evangel is the same feeling Cash would later experience—an awe, almost fear, at being in the presence of the Spirit of God. She was so overpowered that halfway through the service she left by the back door and headed for home. But she couldn't stay away from Evangel, and a few weeks later she committed her life to Christ and began singing in the alto section of the church choir and worked with evangelism and the youth ministry.[3]

Joanne's enthusiasm spread around her family, and especially to Rosey—June's daughter and Cash's new stepdaughter—who would begin attending Evangel and soon encouraging

Johnny and June to do the same.

"I had to realize that it was the prayers of a lot of people that pulled me through [my drug habit]," Cash admitted. "And so I felt like it must be for a purpose—that God had some purpose on earth for me. So when June and I got married, we decided to do things differently. We had both been converted when we were younger, but we'd given our bodies to the devil, and we'd really been through hell. So we decided to try to go back—to try to feel that touch of God we'd felt so long before."

So the pair visited lots of different churches in cities they passed through on tour, and they also went to lots of churches in Hendersonville and Madison, looking for a place they could be comfortable and really feel God.

"The first time we went into [Evangel] we felt the Spirit of God," Cash noted. "I don't know, maybe it scared us a little. The singing and the preaching and the praying were very emotional, and you could just tell it ran deep and was sincere. But, you know, a lot of people get a little scared when they get around the Spirit like that, and maybe that's what happened to us. Anyway, we didn't go back there for a long time."[4]

## NEW LIFE

Cash took yet another step on the road toward a deeper, closer relationship with God just a few days after March 3, 1970—the birthday of John Carter Cash (his only son with June). That's when his life "flip-flopped," according to bassist Marshall Grant.[5]

And before Johnny and June left the hospital with their newest addition, they stopped in the chapel—and the still-newlywed husband and wife knelt with their newborn son and dedicated John Carter to Jesus Christ.

With the Spirit seeming to move powerfully around the Cash and Carter camps, with new life springing up all around them, Johnny and June finally began to attend Evangel Temple regularly early in 1971.

Their experience this time at Evangel was different. For Cash—whose only memories of Pentecostal churches were negative—the worship proved warm, peaceful, and inviting. "I understood that these people were really worshiping," he said. "But there wasn't the frenzy I'd remembered [as a kid]. Instead, there was joy. I stood silently and watched the congregation. They were singing softly. Some of their hands were raised, and their faces showed a quiet bliss. 'This is the real thing,' I felt. 'An off-the-fence kind of worshiping.' They weren't concerned with what the person in the next pew was thinking."[6]

Pastor Snow and Cash quickly became close friends, and one day Cash asked him to come out to his house in Hendersonville—Cash had something to show Snow. In the woods surrounding the Cash estate was an old shack, and there Cash spent hours searching himself, seeking God, and wrestling with doubts and weaknesses he wanted to overcome in order to completely surrender to Christ. Cash explained that the shack was his private place of prayer, and he'd come to a decision recently to follow Jesus Christ closely and allow him to do things through his life.

"He asked me to dedicate that shack to the Lord," Snow said

later, "and we knelt right out there and prayed together. When we did, God's Spirit met with us and confirmed the experience we had there. I could really feel God."[7]

But Snow believed Cash's experience with God should be a permanent and strong one, so he urged him to make a public dedication to God. Snow didn't doubt that Cash was indeed turning his whole life over to the service of God, but that it would be even more wonderful to make that commitment a public one, in God's house.

So, on May 9, 1971, Cash answered Snow's altar call—the pastoral appeal to congregants to come forward and make their lives right with God. Cash stepped into the aisle and walked a few short steps to the wooden altar.

Snow met him there. Cash told him, "I want to live my life right, and the first thing I've got to do is be a spiritual leader in my own home. I'm reaffirming my faith. I'll make the stand, and in case I've had any reservations up to now, I pledge that I'm going to try harder to live as God wants, and I'd like to ask your prayers and the prayers of these people."[8] June slipped from her seat and joined Johnny, and they knelt there between the pastor and the church, full of worshipers, and sealed their rededication to God.

"I don't have a career anymore," Cash declared. "What I have now is a ministry. Everything I have, and everything I do, is given completely to Jesus Christ now. I've lived all my life for the devil up 'til now, and from here on I'm going to live it for the Lord."[9]

Later Pastor Snow said in amazement, "It is one thing for a public figure to join a church; it is another thing for him to humble himself enough to get down on his knees and crawl and cry in front of a congregation."[10]

"I guess I've committed every sin there is to commit," Cash later said. "And I know what it's like on the other side of the street. I know what's good for a man and what's bad for a man. I know what will break up a marriage. I know what will ruin a home. I know what will tear up a man's life. And I'm not going to have any of that stuff around anymore."[11]

## COMMITMENT

Cash was now a member of Evangel Temple. He was connected to a group of Christians—something missing from his life ever since he left Dyess. Of course Cash had visited churches during his adult life, and true, he did commit to the Rev. Gressett's church in Ventura in the early '60s. But this was a different animal altogether. Cash's connection to Evangel was a giant leap forward for him and June—a dramatic statement of faith, one that announced very publicly his desire to serve God. And he did it all clear-eyed and sober—a first since his mid-20s.

"I'm part of you now," Cash told Snow, "and I want to do my share. Just use me and abuse me—anything I can do for the Lord, I want to do it." That also meant financial support, Cash said. Paying tithes was something he wanted to do "just like you expect everyone else to do."

But Snow refused, taking Cash aback. His reasons, however, were valid. "I said, 'Man, you'll wreck my whole church if you do that! If the word gets out that you're paying tithes here, people will think we've got it made. Nobody else will ever give a dime.'"[12] The matter was settled; Cash would contribute in other ways—mostly musical.

But word quickly spread around Nashville that Cash was now a member, and that concerned both Cash and Snow. Are people going to arrive in droves to the door of the church on Sunday morning—jockeying for position, staking out their turf, all to get the best view of Johnny? Will people choose Evangel as their home church because Cash is there now? A sign was placed in the lobby to mitigate things: "Absolutely No Autographs or Pictures Taken Inside the Sanctuary."

But as it turned out, congregants (and outsiders) left Cash alone for the most part. "It's probably the only church in the world where John can come and worship and not be bothered by people," sister Joanne said.

Cash thought so, too. "I can be pretty much be myself at Evangel Temple. I'm just 'old home folks' to the people there, and they don't pay much attention to me. Oh, every now and then somebody will come up to me at church and try to pitch a song to me ... One time a fella walked up before service and pushed a tape into my hand ... [he] said he was a songwriter and wanted me to listen to his stuff. I grabbed him by the arm, marched him right down front, and sat him on the bench. He had to listen to the whole sermon right there. I think the Lord did something for him that day, you know. I think he got something he didn't come looking for."[13]

## BILLY GRAHAM

During this time of transition—as Cash was becoming a public ambassador for Christ—he had a huge ally in Billy Graham, perhaps the most respected religious figure of the twentieth century (and beyond).

"[Graham] and I spent a lot of time talking the issues over, and we determined that I wasn't called to be an evangelist," Cash revealed. "That was work for people other than me. He had advised me to keep singing 'Folsom Prison Blues' and 'A Boy Named Sue' and all those other outlaw songs if that's what people wanted to hear. And then, when it came time to do a gospel song, give it everything I had. Put my heart and soul into all my music, in fact; never compromise; take no prisoners."

"Don't apologize for who you are and what you've done in the past," Graham told Cash. "Be whom you are, and do what you do."[14]

Those were refreshing words for the Man in Black—he wasn't descended upon by a preacher and told to discard the craft that made him famous as a "sacrifice" to God. Instead, Cash was encouraged to use his talents in ways that promoted the Gospel.

"[Graham] said the kids were not going to church, that they were losing interest in religion," Cash remembered about that first meeting, "and he said he thought that the music had a lot to do with it, because there was nothing in the church house that they heard that they liked. The latest thing that the kids can hear in church is 'Bringing in the Sheaves' and 'How Great Thou Art,' and those are not the kinds of things going on in religion that makes the kids say, 'Hey, I like that. Let's go hear some more.' There's nothing that they can relate to. So he talked to me about myself and other songwriters like Kris [Kristofferson] who think along that line, and he kinda challenged me to challenge others to try to use what talent we have to … inspire people to sit up and take notice of religion and Jesus. Well, first thing that happened, the night after he left, I wrote 'What Is Truth'":[15] *A young man of seventeen in Sunday school/ Being taught the golden rule/ And by the time another year has gone around/ It may be his turn to lay his life down/ Can you blame the voice of youth for asking/ 'What is truth.'*[16]

In addition, Graham never used their friendship to curry favor from Cash—in fact it was Cash who volunteered his and June's services to Graham's crusades. Graham, of course, readily accepted—and after working a few of the events, the Cashes decided they'd appear with Graham whenever he asked.

"I've always been able to share my secrets and problems with Billy," Cash emphasized, "and I've benefited greatly from his support and advice. Even during my worst times, when I've fallen back into using pills of one sort or another, he's maintained his friendship with me and given me his ear and his advice, always based solidly on the Bible. He's never pressed me when I've been in trouble; he's waited for me to reveal myself, and then he's helped me as much as he can."[17]

## TAKING IT TO THE STREETS

Buoyed by Graham's encouragement and fired up about his recommitment to God, Cash got bolder with his concert schedule—strategic even. After all, he was performing for Jesus and His glory now, not his own.

Cash was ready to take his music and message to Las Vegas.

It was a strange marriage at first, as Cash never liked the city—even in his most destructive states of mind he called it "Sodom and Gomorrah" and didn't set foot there.

But that attitude changed in the early '70s. "After I got acquainted with the Lord," Cash revealed, "I began to realize that, now that I have something to give those people, Las Vegas is exactly where I should go. So I agreed to play the Hilton International showroom the week of Easter—and while I was entertaining, tell the people something about Jesus."[18]

And, as usual for Cash, his approach was different from the Las Vegas "formula"—a performance to-do list that's almost never violated: he had no comedy preceding him, no orchestra to accompany his band, none of the fancy clothes that had become a trademark for anybody working the rooms in Sin City.

Then when he came to the final five minutes of each show, things really got intense. Cash sang brief excerpts from Christian songs while pictures of Jesus were projected onto the wall behind him, and he quietly confessed to the crowd his love for the Lord.

Not your typical cabaret atmosphere.

Standing-room-only crowds filled the venue three times each night, and the crowds left the room sobered and provoked. Some were angry, but most just had some important things to think about. The hotel management was skeptical at first, but soon warmed to Cash's madness, even purchasing a full-page ad in Nashville's *The Tennessean* urging Cash to accept a return engagement.

Reviews of Cash's performances were stellar. *The Los Angeles Times* called it "a triumph of the highest order" and praised Cash as a man of "deep integrity and purpose ... Unwilling to compromise with the Las Vegas showroom tradition ... Rarely have we seen an opening with such emotional impact," the lengthy review concluded.

Cash knew he was exactly where God wanted him to be, and doing exactly what he thought God expected of him. "I'd give my testimony in the filthiest club in the country—as a matter of fact, I'd enjoy the opportunity," Cash declared. "If I keep on, I know the devil's going to get mad, and I'm ready for it. I expect someone to throw something at me or take a shot at me in a situation like that one of these days.

"But my testimony doesn't offend people, because I tell it in love, and I don't put people down with it. I'm not dogmatic when I testify, I just tell people how I feel and leave it at that ... I just make it a part of my concert and then tell them, 'This is what I love most.' I think Jesus would do something like that. He had more love for the sinner than He did for the hypocrite."[19]

Still, the barbs came Cash's way. "I got as much criticism for playing Las Vegas, consorting with the whores and gamblers, as I did for doing prison concerts," Cash noted incredulously. "My response was that the Pharisees said the same thing about Jesus: 'He dines with publicans and sinners.' The apostle Paul said, 'I will become all things to all men in order that I might win some for Christ now.' I don't have Paul's calling—I'm not out there being all things to all men to win them for Christ—but sometimes I can be a signpost. Sometimes I can sow a seed. And post-hole diggers and seed sewers are mighty important in the building of the kingdom."[20]

## THE HOLY SPIRIT ... AND CONTROVERSY

In the fall of 1971, Cash called Snow and asked him for a meeting at the church. The topic? Cash wanted prayer so he could receive the gift of tongues. The two met with a group of Evangel Temple men, and Cash was then and there baptized in the Holy Spirit. Since that time Cash has described his infilling of the Spirit as a growing, vital source of strength and direction.[21]

But almost a year later, Cash picked up a copy of the *The Tennessean* one morning and saw a headline staring back at him: "Cash Denies Baptism, Altar Call."

Huh?

Cash was compelled to write a letter of clarification to the paper, and it ran the very next day. "I was asked if I had received the baptism of the Holy Spirit on stage at Las Vegas, and if I gave an altar call. The answer was 'no'—but I didn't mean that the Holy Spirit wasn't alive in me and guiding me.[22]

"For a Christian to say the Holy Spirit does not dwell in him is to deny that he is a child of God, and I do not deny that I am a child of God. I am eager to tell it. I feel the Holy Spirit dwells in me at all times. Sometimes it's like a grain of mustard seed, but it's there, and at times, like when we sing those gospel songs, I think it does shine through me."[23]

## COUNTING THE COSTS

Once Cash was asked if he ever feels that his career was damaged by his religious practices: "Not one bit," he replied. "I'm not giving up any aspect of my career. As far as losing my following or something like that—well that doesn't worry me at all."[24]

Still, the consequences of Cash's declarations of faith and end-of-show altar calls were severe in some circles—it didn't manifest itself simply through lost record sales, but also through some of the reaction of religious people, believe it or not, which ranged from attempts to use Cash for their own purposes all the way to condemnations and exclusions from their particular folds. "But I've never regretted speaking up, and I believe that when I get to the Pearly Gates, that's one of the trials God might have in mind if He were to say, 'Come on in, J.R. You've been faithful in a few things.'"[25]

Here's an example of Cash's outspokenness—directed toward the younger generation of the late '60s and early '70s, not long after his rededication to Christ: "They're not coming to understand the real truths of Christianity. They're looking for Jesus in drugs, and He ain't there. Because drugs are the tools of the devil—that's the way I see them ... They've got to have some kind of foundation and moral principle to their lives. And I think they can find it in the Bible ... they don't have to relate to all the bad things that have been done in the name of Christianity ... All this killing in the name of Christ—death to the infidels!—but kids don't have to relate to that crap.'"[26]

## ONE YOUNG PERSON'S REACTION

Her name was Gwen, a student from North Carolina, who was on her way home from Expo '72 in Dallas—a massive evangelical event featuring Billy Graham and gospel-oriented musicians ... including Cash.

For the first time in her life, she was learning how great it was to be a Christian, and she met lots of exciting people in Dallas and had never dreamed there were so many young Christians in the country.

"I guess the guy that really zonked me out the most was Johnny Cash," she revealed. "He was there with his whole group and sang right before Billy Graham preached. Man, Cash was really something! He told how much it meant to him to be a Christian, and quoted Scripture verses between songs. When he sang, he got that whole place to jumping!" Then she paused.

"Come to think of it, I never have thought of Johnny Cash as a Christian before," Gwen admitted. "Isn't he supposed to be a pretty rough guy? I mean, back a few years ago, didn't he drink a lot and do dope or something?"[27]

More than you'll ever know, Gwen.

CHAPTER ELEVEN

# GOSPEL ROAD

*"The devil has plenty of movies these days ... I felt like I was obliged to make one for Jesus."*[1]
—Johnny Cash on the conception of *Gospel Road*

WHILE THE JOHNNY CASH SHOW RAN its course and ended its host's brief television career, it was anything but a black mark on Cash's professional life. In fact, he had more options at his feet than ever—and was busier than ever: Cash could have intensified his involvement at Evangel Temple, helping Rev. Snow and the congregation reach out to the Nashville music industry; he could have jumped into the tour bus till the cows came home, raking in the biggest concert fees of his career and expanding his wildly diverse, populous fan base—or he could have just bowed out for a while and retreated to his rural estate in Hendersonville, Tennessee.

Cash chose none of the above.

Instead of traveling a familiar, well-worn path, the Man in Black decided to blaze a new one. (No surprise.)

And it started with a dream. One of June's.

Turns out she awoke one morning after a fitful night with a vivid, indelible image in her mind: Johnny standing high on a mountaintop in Israel, talking about Jesus. And for Cash, that was the clincher—the final, major portent in a long line of signs that pointed unmistakably to 1973's *Gospel Road*, a major motion picture on the life of Christ financed completely by Johnny and June and shot on location in Israel.

(Some of the other signs Cash had been observing over the years included a visit to Israel in 1966 later followed by his intense periods of Bible study and scholarship on the history of the Church. It all "drew me so powerfully into the story of Christ's three-year ministry ... that I began to feel almost compelled to retell the story in my own words.")[2]

Cash called *Gospel Road* the "most ambitious project I ever attempted," admitting however that he "began writing with no clear picture of where I was going or what, if anything, I would do with the result."[3] While the original concept was filming Cash talking about Jesus as he walked in the places the Son of God himself traveled, by the time the writing was finalized in late 1971, the idea was expanded to include dramatization and music.[4]

In prepping for his script writing, Cash burrowed deeply into Scripture to learn all he could about Jesus. "I dug into the Gospels every day," he recalled, "and then got into the Old Testament—Daniel, Micah, Isaiah, all the prophets. With my rededication, I began to really know Jesus rather than just know about Him. I began to feel Him. My life changed, and my script continued to change as I worked. That was a wonderful experience. Every day it seems like I would find something about Jesus I hadn't known before. I got so excited as I worked, sometimes I'd call Brother [Jimmy] Snow on the phone just to tell him what I was finding out."[5]

To some observers, however, the project was a head-scratcher: What, exactly, was Cash thinking? Half a million bucks out of his pocket? A crew of forty to feed and house? Next to no dialogue, save for Cash's foreboding, baritone-drenched narration? A soundtrack of country sounds instead of the safe, traditional orchestral approach? (And … a blond Jesus?)

But the project had nothing to do with cost or artistic acceptance or marketability; it had everything to do, rather, with Cash's singular, God-driven vision that would suffer no outside interference, no matter what. "I wanted to do it the way I felt led to do it," he explained, "and if I had called in other people to finance it, I would have had to let them help edit it, too … I've made a lot of big money, and I think God let that happen for a purpose. It's God's money anyway—He's just letting me use it to make a film about Jesus." (Cash diverted all profits to charity as well.)[6]

"John is trying to bring his Jesus to the whole world," director Robert Elfstrom said after production wrapped. "When I would improvise something like picking up a rock and tossing it, Johnny would say, 'My Jesus wouldn't do that.' It's very personal for John."[7]

"Lots of people go all their lives thinking Jesus was some kind of pious pushover," Cash said, explaining *Gospel Road*'s approach. "He's been portrayed as a sissy, and I'm just not buying that concept of Him. He didn't bawl on that cross: I think if you or I had been up there we would've squalled and bawled and tried to get down. Not Jesus. He was a real man. He walked into the seat of authority—Him just a man of the street—and called the Pharisees 'hypocrites' to their faces. That takes a real man, too."[8]

## "LIKE GOING HOME"

"You see, for somebody like me who grew up singing Jesus songs all his life and who was raised up in a Baptist Church, going to Israel is like going home," Cash noted concerning the fringe benefits of filming in the Promised Land. "You see the things you've been singing about all your life, and you go home, and there it is. You want to hug it.[9]

"Even now I am drawn like a prodigal son to the land," Cash noted. Tellingly, he paused production long enough to be baptized by immersion in the Jordan River.[10]

## AN INSIDE VIEW

Thirty years after *Gospel Road* hit movie houses across the country, the film understandably doesn't play today like something Twentieth Century Fox would distribute—but it likely turned a few heads in the early '70s. That's mostly due to the fact that its release coincided with the Jesus Movement, a cultural phenomenon that couched Christ as a hippie-loving Son of God; not much of a stretch, as the Jesus everybody imagined then (and now) is longhaired, bearded, possesses a thrift-store wardrobe, and clearly espouses love—just like the hippie kids. The Jesus Movement certainly helped *Godspell* and *Jesus*

*Christ Superstar*. So it's easy to imagine *Gospel Road*—with its ragtag cadre of vagabond extras, close-to-the-cradle-of-creation setting, and prominent placement of Cash as a black-clad, Bible-toting narrator, ever popular with the younger generation as well as more traditional folks—also appealing to Jesus Movement adherents.

The sparse production (shot on cheaper 16 millimeter film as opposed to the standard 35 millimeter) leans heavily on smart, frequent edits, the panorama of the Israeli countryside (including a compelling slo-mo shot flying just above the winding Jordan River), and Cash's foreboding, gut-level narration and left-turn hillbilly tunes that provide nearly the only soundtrack. June Carter Cash, who portrays Mary Magdalene, offers the only real dialogue in an emotional portrayal of the ex-prostitute and close friend of the Messiah. June, in fact, trained for two years at New York's Neighborhood Playhouse in the 1950s—and the fact that her five-minute scene where Jesus cleanses her is "the emotional peak of the show" makes total sense.[11]

Where *Gospel Road* falters a bit is in the portrayal of Jesus. Cash & Co. had planned all along to film only Jesus' hands and feet—a gutsy, more abstract proposition. But literally the night before filming began it was decided to draft director Elfstrom into the role of Christ—and all of him, not just his hands and feet. But with his full, Grizzly Adams' beard and stringy blonde hair, Elfstrom stands out from the rest of the darker, more middle-Eastern looking cast—but for all the wrong reasons. He "often looks like a figure from a Baptist calendar come eerily to life" noted one critic.[12]

*Gospel Road* wins, however, through Cash's thunderous voice of a twentieth-century prophet. His words are the common thread weaving scenes together, filling them with context, and adorning them with believability. Here the Man in Black, in his most overt declaration of faith yet, communicates and inspires a range of emotions. The opening shot, for example—which took place, as June dreamed, on the summit of Mount Arable, overlooking Galilee—is a sweeping, grand introduction to Cash's at once folk-hero and evangelical vision of Jesus and His ministry that sets the stage for the rest of the film.

## LITTLE SIGNS

Cash pointed out that the intensity of the month-long production schedule was buoyed by a steady succession of little blessings and signs that God was indeed smiling on the proceedings.

"When we got to the Church of the Beatitudes, which we'd been told was closed, the custodian was there with the key," Cash remembered incredulously. "He'd just had a feeling, he said, that somebody was going to need to film in the church, so he'd come and waited for us. And while it didn't rain for 29 of our 30 days in the Holy Land, it did rain a little, just enough, on the only day we needed it, just as we were shooting the scene in which Jesus calms the storm on the Sea of Galilee. Every way we turned, doors opened—some that had been closed, some we didn't even know were there … it seemed strange, mysterious, often almost magical."[13]

One of the driver-guides was chummy with many offices in the Israeli government, and even though his car's license plates identified him as an Arab, he could go anywhere and get anything done. Another driver was a veteran of the Israeli army and was skilled at getting Cash into restricted areas like the Golan Heights, where the fiercest battles of the Six-Day War had been fought.

In need of twelve disciples, they placed an ad in the *Jerusalem Post* describing what was required, and about fifty young men came to the hotel lobby. Big mix of nationalities—Swedes, Danes, Germans, Swiss, French, British, Americans—as well as an assortment of "dropouts, draft resisters, seekers, adventurers, and escapees from something or other, some of them half starved and sleeping in the streets, none of them with money or means—and it wasn't hard at all to find the faces of our disciples in their ranks."[14]

## THE SOUNDTRACK

Cash credited Billy Graham for helping to inspire the musical part of *Gospel Road* when one day he wondered with Cash if there were songwriters who could do songs on Jesus as well as the best ones in the business—and that's what Cash did, recruiting the likes of Joe South, John Denver, Larry Gatlin, Christopher Wren, and Kris Kristofferson.[15]

In fact, one of the biggest surprises for Cash came from his friend and fellow songwriter Kristofferson, who composed a song for the *Gospel Road* soundtrack after attending a service at Evangel Temple—a shock as Cash already knew Kristofferson's spirituality was quite different than his.

Regardless, Kristofferson recalled that when Pastor Snow asked people who felt lost to raise their hands. "My head was saying, 'That'll be the day that I raise my hand in front of a bunch of strangers,' but my hand went up anyhow," Kristofferson remembered. "I couldn't see if anyone else's did because we all had our heads bowed, but then Jimmy asked people who'd raised their hands to walk up to the front of the church. I said there was no way in hell I was going to do that, but I found myself doing it. He asked if I was ready to accept Jesus Christ, and I said I don't know, I didn't know what I was doing there. He said something about forgiveness, and I completely fell apart, was crying uncontrollably, but it felt like this whole darkness was lifted off my shoulders ... "[16]

After that experience, Kristofferson wrote the famous country dirge, "Why Me," as well as a tune that would make it onto the soundtrack, "Burden of Freedom."

And that's when Cash got the image in his head of Jesus—accompanied by "Burden of Freedom"—carrying His cross, falling, struggling, making the long, torturous journey to Calvary.[17]

## IT'S SHOWTIME!

When the Cashes finally screened *Gospel Road* for Billy and Ruth Graham at the Cash spread, Graham wanted to distribute it, pretty much on the spot. "We've never distributed a film that we didn't produce ourselves," wrote Graham in his autobiography. "But Word Wide Pictures must distribute *Gospel Road*. We know its audience."[18]

The movie was an instant success through Word Wide, with hundreds of copies being shown to packed churches every week, week after week, year round. Many hundreds have made a commitment to Christ during Graham's filmed invitation at the end of the picture.[19]

"[*Gospel Road*] has been one of the best evangelistic film tools that the Billy Graham Evangelistic Association has had," Graham added, "with hundreds of prints in circulation. Missionaries are using it in video vans in Africa, India, and elsewhere."[20]

"I really wanted to zero in on Christ," Cash noted. "I had never seen a film on Christ that I could relate to, one that was really believable." And yet, being a devout evangelical Christian, Cash sees his film as a statement of personal faith rather than as a vehicle for proselytizing. "Jesus has been the most important thing in our lives these past six years. And this film is the proudest work of my career. It's the reason I'm on this earth."[21]

CHAPTER TWELVE

# MEETING THE MAN IN WHITE

JOHNNY CASH REACHED A CRITICAL PEAK OF commercial success and popularity in the late '60s and early '70s, boasting an uncommonly wide range of fans while his rootsy flair fit like a glove over the bourgeoning singer-songwriter glut on AM radio.

But as the 1970s wore on—and throughout the 1980s—Cash's star waned, blinked, and fluttered. This period was an odd, mixed bag of few triumphs and inconsistent success commercially and artistically, and further marred by small drug relapses, new health problems, a traumatic armed robbery at the Cash estate on Christmas Day in Jamaica, and a growing sense that the Man in Black's best musical days were far behind him.

It started in 1974 when Columbia brass convinced him to sing tunes chosen by outside producers. Cash called the album

*John R. Cash*, the low point of his recording career. Others followed, including gospel collections such as 1975's *Precious Moments*, dedicated to his late brother Jack, and 1979's *A Believer Sings the Truth*, an extensive double album with many overdubs that took an unusually long time (six months) to complete. In the latter year, two very different organizations saw fit to honor Cash: He received the Humanitarian Award from the United Nations, and Youth for Christ—a nationwide organization committed to youth ministry—named him Man of the Year.

Cash continued to draw big crowds on the concert circuit, though—a fact that never changed much throughout his career, no matter how healthy he was or how strongly his creative juices were flowing in the studio. Fans dug nothing more than seeing Cash take the stage and air out his world-weary baritone over his famous chigga-chigga rhythm. And although it wasn't getting the marquee attention of a few years earlier, Cash's faith in Christ remained resolute and strident, and he was even more confident that the entertainment industry could be the "front lines for spiritual battles."

"There's a decline of morals all around," he said in an interview before a show in New York in 1976. "The country is just not in the best shape. Churches are losing members every day. People are backsliding ... I'm not saying we can change the world, but you can't listen to our show without seeing the strength and influence of the family unit. When we sing 'Will the Circle Be Unbroken?' that isn't just a song, it's our life. God and family—the simple old traditional values that hold a person together."[1]

But even the media—with nothing really newsworthy about Cash to fill pages and tiring of his populist-patriotic-religious-rural persona in the face of what was becoming a wild decade without him—began looking elsewhere. In his book *Country*, Nick Tosches came down heavy on Cash:

"Johnny Cash and his God are a particularly tedious act. The strongest drink Cash serves at his parties is non-alcoholic fruit punch ... Each year, Johnny Cash's mind seems to grow more monomaniacal. His 1976 hit, 'Sold Out of Flagpoles,' was an absurd mess of godly patriotism, a song berserk with blandness and as dumb as any in the 1975 film *Nashville*."[2]

As he entered the 1980s, the advent of image-conscious MTV didn't help Cash, either. He did manage to form a veritable country music super group with Willie Nelson, Waylon Jennings, and Kris Kristofferson in 1985—the Highwaymen. But the success garnered by Cash and his pals—also rebellious figures who bucked the Nashville bulls, doing as they pleased, musically and otherwise—was unfortunately the exception for Cash, not the rule. He also recorded a gospel album for Word Records in 1986, *Believe in Him*.

But the final, overall toll was a recording career that lacked the direction and fire of years past.

According to Cash chronicler Michael Streissguth, his music of this period "lacked the authority, the desperation, the closeness to the earth that defined the music that Cash first offered to America in the 1950s."[3]

Even Cash acknowledged (years after the fact) that he lost his way musically during this time: "It got off track, yeah," he told *Rolling Stone*'s Steve Pond. "There were times when I didn't care. It was, like, complete apathy from the record company, and I guess I got that way, too. Finally, we both agreed that we weren't entertaining each other anymore. When they said, 'Let's start talking about renewing the contract,' I said: 'Let's face it, nobody down here wants me. Nobody's interested in producing me or trying to sell my records. I'll go somewhere else, thank you very much.'"[4]

With that, Columbia Records did the unthinkable: After more than a quarter century partnering with a living legend, the label dropped Johnny Cash from its roster in 1986.

## FALLING OFF THE WAGON

Cash had eye surgery in 1981 and continued taking painkillers after it was necessary. But he suffered his first major relapse into drug addiction because of ... an ostrich.

In 1983, it seems Cash was walking around his exotic animal park he'd set up on the grounds of The House of Cash when he was confronted by an angry, eight-foot ostrich that hissed aggressively at him. Later he was faced with the same ostrich again, but this time Cash was prepared: As the ostrich advanced toward him, presumably to attack, Cash swung a huge stick at his neck—and hit nothing but air. The surprisingly nimble ostrich leaped over the errant stick and landed on Cash's torso, breaking four of his ribs and causing an abdominal tear down to his belt buckle.

Doctors stitched Cash back up, but he was in a lot of pain. So once again, those demon painkillers were prescribed. And they led to sleeping pills. Which led to "uppers" again. Soon Cash was off the wagon. Things went on that way for a while until he fell and broke his kneecap, which led to more strong painkillers, enough to last for a scheduled tour of England, as well as sleeping pills (in case the pain kept Cash from sleeping) and "uppers" (to kill the effects of the sleeping pills when it was time to perform). The chemical combo gave Cash blackouts—to wit, he performed in fourteen cities, but he only remembered four gigs.

"So there I was," Cash recalled. "Up and running, strung out, slowed down, sped up, turned around, hung on the hook, having a ball, living in hell. Before long I began to get the impression that I was in trouble ... but kept going anyway. The idea of taking things to their logical conclusion, just drugging and drinking until I slipped all the way out of this world, began to dance quietly around the back of my mind. That was weirdly comforting."[5]

In Nottingham, England, Cash was hallucinating and became convinced that a Murphy bed was inside a bedroom wall. Despite June's protests, Cash tore at that wall until the paneling broke open, showering old dirt and splinters into his right hand—which was quite bloody by the time Cash admitted his drug-influenced faux pas.[6]

By the time Cash came home, he not only needed surgery on his hand, he was also bleeding internally. The truckloads of pills he was taking literally burned holes in his stomach—and although he got the necessary fourteen units of blood to replace what he'd lost, there was no other option except an operation. Under the knife, doctors removed Cash's duodenum, parts of his stomach and spleen, and several feet of intestine.

In spite of Cash's newest life-threatening situation, he was so far gone that he actually sneaked drugs into the hospital—a stash of Percodans, amphetamines, and Valium—in a sack tied to the back of the television in his room. Cash hid the Valium under the bandages covering the incision on his belly. "I managed to pull the dressing up and get them snugged in there, safe and sound," Cash recalled ruefully. "I thought I'd been really clever.[7]

"Many times I was aware enough to pray, and many times, in my pain and mental terror, I felt that warm presence of the Great Healer, and I always knew that I would live, and that I wasn't finished for Him yet," Cash remembered. "Once when I was unconscious, I suddenly became aware of a gentle hand on my forehead and I heard my mother's voice. 'Lord,' she said, 'You took one of my boys, and if You're going to take this one, he's Yours to take, but I ask you, let him live and teach him to serve You better. Surely You still have work for him to do.'"[8]

## INTERVENTION

Cash realized at that point that he hated himself. "Mine wasn't a soft-core, pop-psychology self-hatred," Cash noted. "It was profound, a violent, daily holocaust of revulsion, shame, and one way or another it had to stop. I couldn't stand it any longer. So when the intervention came, it was welcome. As my friends and family spoke, I was telling myself, 'This is it. This is my salvation. God has sent these people to show me a way out. I'm going to get a chance to live.'"

Cash's family and closest friends met with a doctor, and together they laid it all on the line for Cash—he had to clean up. No two ways about it. "I'm still absolutely convinced that the intervention was the hand of God working in my life, telling me that I still had a long way to go, a lot left to do,"

Cash said. "The amazing encouragement I got, the [testimonies] of all those people, made me believe in myself again. But first I had to humble myself before God. I was going to the Betty Ford Center."[9]

Cash entered the Betty Ford Center in 1984. After about three weeks, he started coming to life again, feeling refreshed … even reborn. Betty Ford herself gave a daily talk that Cash attended, and his counselor was "hard-nosed and very effective. He wouldn't give me an inch, and he got the job done with me. Neither I nor any of the other celebrities got any breaks in any way, especially not in the process of education and self-discovery, basically a concentrated twelve-step program that's the core of the treatment. I wasn't allowed to get away with anything but 'rigorous honesty.'[10]

"[Mine is] an ongoing struggle," Cash later admitted. "I do know, though, that if I commit myself to God every morning and stay honest with Him and myself, I make it through the day just beautifully."[11]

## MEETING THE MAN IN WHITE

The last of Cash's correspondence courses on the Bible was on the life of St. Paul the Apostle. "Paul fascinated me greatly," Cash said, "and eventually the thought occurred to me that I could do with his story what I had done with that of Jesus in *Gospel Road*: tell it my way for my own benefit and that of anyone else who might be interested. Writing a novel was something I'd never done, so that's the form I chose."[12]

This thought process began in 1977. But despite some promising starts, Cash's lack of inspiration and bout with drugs in the early '80s put it on the shelf indefinitely. "Only occasionally would I take it out and try to write," Cash remembered. "Mood-altering drugs vex the spirit, and if inspiration comes to a writer while under the influence, it's usually distorted, meaningless, and senseless by the time it gets on paper."[13]

Cash let Billy Graham read his unfinished portions, and Graham always asked Cash if the book was finished. Cash would reply that he was busy on the road, et cetera.

Deep inside, though, Cash wanted to get a sense of what Paul saw on the Damascus Road—the vision that turned his life around. From the pulpit at a Billy Graham crusade, Cash heard the evangelist tell the huge crowd that Johnny Cash had written a book about Paul called *Man in White*, and that it was one of the best writings on Paul he'd ever read. Cash was embarrassed and ashamed. *Man in White* was about halfway done, and Paul was still in limbo on the Damascus Road.

But something would change all of that.

Ray Cash died in 1985, at the age of eighty-eight. At the end of his life, Ray Cash mellowed a lot and turned into a sweet, kind soul.[14]

The night before his father's funeral, Cash fell asleep and had a vivid dream. He was in front of his parents' house, alone, facing the road, when a massive bright silver limo crested over the hill and stopped in front of the house. There was no driver, but a door swung open, and Cash's daddy exited the vehicle and started walking toward his son. Ray Cash was wearing the exact funeral garb that his family chose for him—a blue suit, white silk shirt, and burgundy tie. He was smiling, bounding toward Johnny with a youthful spring in his step. In fact, everything about him looked younger: his eyes, his teeth, his hair. He was a new man.

Then Cash said to his daddy, "I was waiting for you to come home," and reached out for a handshake. Ray's hand reached out as well, but before they could shake, a long row of light shot up from the ground between them. Ray smiled like he knew what was up, and he dropped his hand and simply looked at Johnny. The light separating them widened, grew in brilliance, and became impossible to cross.

Cash looked through the window of the house, and although he couldn't see his momma, he knew she was inside. Cash turned and asked his daddy if he was coming inside. Ray Cash smiled and said no, that he felt that would cause more pain for everybody.

"Tell your mother that I just couldn't come back. I'm so comfortable and happy where I am. I just don't belong here anymore," Ray said.

The light became more intense, and Cash could no longer see his daddy. Then the light was gone, as was Ray.

Cash woke up and peered at the clock through the darkness—1 a.m. He'd been asleep only for a few minutes. Cash was shaken, so he walked and sat up all night, finally finding peace as day broke. Later that day, he took his momma aside and said, "I had a God-sent dream last night … I dreamed about Daddy, and he asked me to tell you … he's comfortable and happy where he is. Besides, he said that he doesn't belong here anymore." She cried, then laughed: "God still has His hand on you."[15]

After Cash's vivid dream about his daddy—and especially the light that overpowered the whole scene—he had a better, more vivid sense of what Paul may have experienced on the Road to Damascus. Inspiration had arrived. The book, in fact, related to the moment the light shone all around Paul. And Cash was able to finish his novel.

For his part, Cash identified with bits and pieces of Paul's life. His conversion was dramatic, and he endured some trials of faith—but he was able to declare, "In any situation I find myself in, I am content because of Jesus Christ." Cash desired that in his own life. "He was a man who always had a mission, who would never stop, who was always going here, going there, starting this, planning that; a life of ease and retirement wasn't on his agenda, just as it isn't on mine," Cash noted. "I'm much more interested in keeping on down the roads I know and whatever new ones might reveal themselves to me, trying to tap that strength Paul found: the power of God that's inside me that's there for me if only I seek it."[16]

## FIRST TASTE OF HEAVEN?

In 1988, Cash was back in the hospital, this time for heart bypass surgery. After the surgery, he contracted double pneumonia and was placed on a respirator. "I was as close to death as you could get," Cash said, adding that he felt himself fading away. "The doctors were saying they were losing me. I was going, and there was that wonderful light that I going into. It was awesome, indescribable—beauty and peace, love and joy—and then all of a sudden, there I was again, all in pain and awake. I was so disappointed.[17]

"My eyes flew open and I saw doctors. I couldn't believe it.

Sorrow welled up in me. I started crying, and then I got so angry that I was sobbing and snarling at the same time. I found my wits and began trying to tell them to let me go, to send me back, but they had a tube down my throat, so I couldn't get it across to them. I gave up trying. I never forgot that light, [though] and it changed me.[18]

"But when I realized a day or so later what point I had been to, I started thanking God for life and thinking only of life … I'm not obsessed with death, I'm obsessed with living. The battle against the dark one and the clinging to the right one is what my life is about."[19]

CHAPTER THIRTEEN

# THE WANDERER

AFTER JOHNNY CASH WAS DROPPED FROM the Columbia label in 1986, he hooked up quite quickly with PolyGram—largely because many of the Columbia execs he knew had done the same thing. Indeed, there's something to be said for common history.

But personnel turnover similarly plagued PolyGram after a few years, and Cash found himself again without advocates in important divisions such as A&R. It's an old story: One of the cardinal, physical laws of the music business is No Support in the Artist & Repertoire Department Equals No Marketing Support, Either—which means your record, no matter how good it is, will likely die in a pile.

Cash's final album with PolyGram was 1991's *The Mystery of Life,* a pretty decent recording based on what Cash knows down deep: cowboys, trains, outlaws, and drifters versus an unsympathetic American landscape. But no one was listening—mostly because nobody heard it. And *The Mystery of Life* indeed died in a pile.[1]

Even with his 1992 induction into the Rock and Roll Hall of Fame and still raking in the box office bucks, Cash was seeing fewer and fewer successes with his albums. “Nobody at [PolyGram] is excited about my recording career. If I hear demographics one more time, I'm gonna puke right in their faces. I mean, I recorded songs that I think are really some of my best work, like the last album, *The Mystery of Life*, but I think they must have pressed a hundred copies and sent 'em out …

“But I don't grieve over it. I mean, hell, I don't lose sleep over not having a record in the charts. But I know that I'm capable of doing a lot better work than I've been doing the last few years, and I want to get into a situation where I can do that.”[2]

## FREIGHT TRAIN TO ZOOROPA

Cash was on tour and scheduled for a show in Dublin. U2 were in the studio cutting 1993's *Zooropa*, the avant-garde follow-up to their megasmash, “dream it all up again” record, *Achtung Baby*. Bono and Adam Clayton had already made the Man in Black's acquaintance a few years before, and there was talk several times about penning a song together. Something tentatively entitled “Ellis Island” was already in the works—but who knew if and when anything would come of it?

This time, though, Bono had a giant coup in mind involving Cash. U2 producers Brian Eno and Flood opposed it, but Bono got his way: How 'bout inviting Cash into the studio while he would be in town to lend some vocals to a track?

According to Cash, here's how it went down: "Three of 'em came [to the Dublin show]: [guitarist] the Edge, and [drummer] Larry Mullen, and Bono. And I got them out onstage with me at the end of the show to sing 'Big River.' That was really quite a party. Bono wrote down his verse in the palm of his hand. He was singin' looking at his hand. 'Course, he had that perpetual cigarette in his other hand. After the show, he asked me if I would come by the studio the next day and listen to a song he wrote for me. And we put down the track that day. I didn't have any idea it was going to be on the album—he says, 'We're just recording some experimental music.'"[3]

The working title of the song Bono had in mind was "Johnny Cash on the Moon." But Bono's lyrical mood was decidedly Book of Ecclesiastes-driven, and the first real title was "The Preacher." But the Edge offered that it would fit better with the rest of the album to call the song "The Wanderer."[4]

Over a loopy, almost playful synth-driven melody mixed with a soft, western-sky cowboy chorus, Cash takes center stage vocally, assuming the role of a preacher on a desperate journey of the flesh. Here Cash is *in search of experience—to taste and touch and to feel as much as a man can before he repents.*[5] Knowledge, sex, mammon, gold, whatever. "The setting is a kind of surreal, post-nuclear *Paris, Texas*, world in which loyalty, faith, and honor have become virtually extinct. Bono had Flannery O'Conner in mind—the way she writes about the strangest American characters and their do-it-yourself religion with humor, sympathy, and love."[6] "The Wanderer" stood out like mad from the rest of the record.

"If you imagine the album being set in this place, Zooropa," Flood reflected, "just when you're expecting the norm to finish the album, you get somebody who's outside the whole thing, wandering through, discussing it. It's like the perfect full stop. It throws a whole different light on the conceptualization of the record."[7]

Significantly, it was Bono who filled the vocal gaps before Cash stepped up to the microphone—but the result was akin to admitting to the public that the glittery façade U2 spent the last two years creating was up in smoke. It just felt off.

The preacher character uses "Jesus' exhortation to leave your wife and children and follow Him as an excuse to skip out on his responsibilities. He is playing with the ancient antinomian heresy that you can sin your way to salvation ... [but] by having Johnny Cash sing the song, Bono erects another false face. The part of the audience that shared his spiritual side (as well as the part that understands how serious a figure Johnny Cash really is) will understand the deeper message, and those who want to think it's camp will just get a kick out of U2 casting Johnny Cash as Hazel Motes."[8]

Further, as the band prepped the track without Cash, the tone of the tune was a complete lark. A huge joke. Nobody took it seriously. "They took on the identity of the ultimate Holiday Inn band from hell and produced an anachronistic noise to match ... until Johnny Cash opens his mouth, that is. The result is awesome and eerie at once, the contrast between the cheap throwaway backing and Cash's monumental delivery lending the whole a thoroughly skewed power that's entirely appropriate."[9]

Still, Cash had reservations. He apparently didn't like singing the line, *I went out for the papers/ Told her I'd be back by noon*. More of Bono's wanderlust, desire to escape, to embrace irresponsible behavior.

"[Cash] used to leave that verse out because he liked it much heavier," Bono remembered. "I always liked that, you know, bottle of milk, newspapers and he's off. He's got God's work to do. He's looking for knowledge as well, and experience. He's on tour."[10]

And so, what was at first an informal studio session became the nitro-fueled catalyst that lit yet another all-important fire under Cash's fading career. "The Wanderer" thrust Cash back into the public eye like a rocket—and not with just any group. This was U2, the biggest, most influential band on the planet. And they gave Cash a plumb cherry spot on *Zooropa*—the closing tune.

It wouldn't be long now before Cash turned heads again—and with his own albums.

CHAPTER FOURTEEN

# AMERICAN RECORDINGS

*"I'd like to do an album called* Johnny Cash: Late and Alone. *I'd like to do really hard songs and gut songs and say things that you don't hear these days. I mean, sing intimate, really intimate things to that woman, you know? Things that my fans would be surprised to hear me say."*[1]
—Johnny Cash in December 1992

RICK RUBIN MADE HIS MARK IN music out of zigging while others were busy zagging. A palefaced, guru-bearded Gotham impresario, in the 1980s he introduced the world to the Beastie Boys and Public Enemy and made Run DMC a household name with *Raising Hell*. Then just when Rubin was getting pigeonholed as a rap guy, he cut and ran with the likes of Slayer, The Cult, and Red Hot Chili Peppers. In other words, don't make the mistake of defining Rubin—he fits into more than just one artistic slot. (Not unlike Johnny Cash.)

On the heels of his much talked about contribution to U2's *Zooropa* album, Cash showed his mettle as a potentially vital player in the game once again. And Rick Rubin knew it better than anybody. He saw something in the old man—a fire that still burned, a soul that still connected to listeners, a deep, rich well of artistry that was timeless, almost primeval.

So in 1993, Rubin visited Cash backstage in Los Angeles and threw his pitch up the flagpole to see if the Man in Black would salute, but the singer was skeptical. "I said, 'So what makes you think you could—you would—do something with me that nobody else has tried or nobody else wants to do?'" Cash recalled. "He said, 'I just want you to take your guitar and sing me some songs, and those are the songs I want to put down on record. Sing me what you love and what you feel good about, and let's record those.'"[2]

Cash hadn't heard that kind of openness to his expression since Miss Mae Fielder gave him voice lessons back in Dyess. What's more, Cash trusted Rubin. So he instructed his manager, Lou Robin, to negotiate a deal, and just like that Cash was added to the stable of American Records artists.

## LIVING ROOM MUSIC

Cash traveled to Hollywood and set up camp in Rubin's house and cut song after song. The duo also bunkered down in Cash's cabin in Hendersonville for more recording. The latter is a quiet, secluded space made of hand-cut pine and fir that Cash christened Cedar Hill Refuge.

"I picked the site 10 years before I had [the cabin] built," Cash revealed. "It was like a prayer, a dedication to this spot of earth where I could have a place of refuge. It restores me. It returns me to nature and God. I come here in pain sometimes and take a few deep breaths and meditate on things. Then the pain goes away, and I relax ... In this cabin I fight the battle inside all of us, common everyday human frailties, things of the flesh. I wrestle with the questions of sin and redemption and try to stay in accord with God's will."[3]

"So I started showing up ... with my guitar, and he had a microphone set up," Cash continued. "I brought a list of songs, and he brought a list. There was no clock on the wall to watch, no red light telling us this was a 'take.'"[4]

By the end of the sessions, they had eighty songs in the can, all with just Cash's voice accompanied by his acoustic guitar. Rubin first supposed the initial recordings as demos—the real album would be recut later—but after hearing their stark, earthy power, Rubin decided to run with Cash's living room music.

"There was just such a purity of hearing him in that light," Rubin noted later. "For all the records he'd made over the years, he'd never really made one like that before. Without that being the plan in advance, it just kind of evolved into, 'Wow, ya know, this really kind of sounds like the record I wish I could get. Ya know, as a fan, this is the one I wish I could go buy.' But, again, it was completely by accident."[5]

"I discovered my own self and what makes me tick musically and what I really like," Cash said. "It was really a great inward journey, doing all these sessions over a period of nine months and Rick sitting there not so much as a producer but as a friend who shared the songs with me. 'What else you got?' he'd say, or 'Listen to this one,' and he'd play one.[6]

"And it was a revelation, because I had always wanted to do an album with just my guitar. I remember 25 years ago telling Marty Robbins I wanted to do an album called *Late and Alone*. But it never felt right. Doing that record was a dream come true."[7]

On *American Recordings*, Cash takes on the role of the brooding, aged wise man—the gentle thunder of his famous baritone sounding all the more apocalyptic, riveting, and weighty with his acoustic guitar only quietly strumming the melodies. The instrument is merely a placeholder. The star of the show is what emanates from Cash's mouth. Here Cash's folk hero status is slowly morphing into icon-land.

What's more, the lyrical mood of the album is lonesome and melancholy—even dark. And no other track on *American Recordings* is so reflective of that fact than "Delia's Gone," a haunting account of domestic homicide. *First time I shot her/ I shot her in the side/ Hard to watch her suffer/ But with the second shot she died/ Delia's gone, one more round Delia's gone* . . .[8]

But Cash approaches "Delia's Gone" with a disarming sense of whimsy, his voice disguising the protagonist's horrible deed and Cash's overall tone and approach belying the dark subject matter. And that's the essence of Cash's artistic range—something listeners would see most clearly during the Cash-Rubin collaboration—his ability to bring something special (even unapproachable) to any song he decided to cover.

"I have to feel like it's my song when I sing it," Cash explained. "It has to be believable. I have to be able to deliver it honestly, whether it's old or new. There's not a song I sing that I don't feel that way about."[9]

Cash also borrows from the likes of Nick Cave ("The Beast in Me"), Tom Waits ("Down There by the Train"), Leonard Cohen ("Bird on a Wire"), Glenn Danzig ("Thirteen"), and Loudon Wainwright III ("The Man Who Couldn't Cry"). The latter, along with Jimmy Driftwood's "Tennessee Stud," was recorded live at the Viper Room, the trendy L.A. watering hole that isn't terribly used to senior citizens taking the stage—much less winning over the youthful crowd. And with most every verse in the aforementioned tunes, the Viper Room audience is tickled and touched, their audible hoops, hollers, and applause welcoming Cash into their MTV-saturated hearts.

## DEATH AND LIFE

After MTV started airing "Delia's Gone"—starring Cash as the killer and then supermodel Kate Moss as Delia—Cash suddenly was dubbed an "O.G." (original gangsta). Seems some observers equated the Cash song with hip-hop tracks that regularly revel in violence. But that's far from the case—after all, by the time the song concludes, the killer was behind bars, haunted by "the patter of Delia's feet." This isn't the bling bling, throwaway, drive-by mayhem; Cash couches it with sobering honesty—as "a bitter, impossible-to-swallow pill."[10]

And while some critics gave Cash flak for things like the explicit death imagery in "Delia's Gone," the Man in Black shrugged it off (as usual).

"There's always been that side of me, and it has been brought to the fore again," Cash noted. "But there's a rebel in all of us ... I wrote a song about shooting a man in Reno just to watch him die ('Folsom Prison Blues'). But I feel if it's a reflection of our culture, it's all right."[11]

But of utmost importance to Cash is communicating the hope of God's love—the hope of salvation—even in the midst of his outlaw, rebellious tunes. Cash exercises his spirituality on *American Recordings* with a cover of Kris Kristofferson's "Why Me Lord," one of the two songs Kristofferson wrote following his "religious experience" at Evangel Temple in the early '70s. And in that vein Cash himself airs out one of his own tracks, the darkly hued, beautifully poetic folk number, "Redemption": *In the deep crimson dew/ The tree of life grew/ And the blood gave life/ To the branches of the tree/ And the blood was the price/ That set the captives free …* [12]

Cash even named the two dogs that appear with him on the cover of *American Recordings*: Sin and Redemption. Sin, he explained to one writer, is the black dog with the white stripe, and Redemption is the white dog with the black stripe. "That's kind of the theme of that album," he added, "and I think it says it for me, too. When I was really bad, I was not all bad. When I was really trying to be good, I could never be all good. There would be that black streak going through."[13]

Fans and critics alike lauded *American Recordings*. Cash was indeed back. He even nabbed a Grammy for Best Contemporary Folk Album.

## ON THE ROAD AGAIN

A rejuvenated Cash hit the concert trail in support of his brand-new album and brand-new "it" artist status. In the meantime, there was a frenzied curiosity about Cash. Tastemakers and paparazzi prey jammed into Cash's club shows, fascinated by this old man's honest, enduring charisma. (And to head off any relapses into drug use, Cash traveled during the tour with a minister who was a recovering drug addict and alcoholic. "He keeps me off the streets," Cash said, "and he counsels everybody on the show who might have a problem, no matter what it is.")[14]

"It started feeling like 1955 again," he noted. "I began playing young people's places like the Fillmore ... I discovered all over again how it felt to play for a crowd of people with no chairs or tables, standing on their feet, jammed together, energizing each other."[15]

The Viper Room, in particular, was "kinda like playing a bloody honky-tonk in the '50s," Cash revealed.[16]

Rubin insisted Cash was terrified at the prospect of playing in front a club crowd—especially when it was just his voice and his acoustic guitar. "It scared him to death," Rubin remembered.[17]

When it was time to perform songs from *American Recordings*, a stool appeared onstage, and Cash broke everything down to his black D28 Martin guitar and his voice. "I learned the trick of making myself feel like the audience was just that one other person late and alone in a room," Cash revealed. "And that, too, was a great pleasure. It was also more than rewarding to find that the young people were eager, perhaps even hungry, for the spiritual songs I've always loved. I'd always prayed that might happen."[18]

CHAPTER FIFTEEN

# UNCHAINED

*"I love songs about horses, railroads, land, judgment day, family, hard times, whiskey, courtship, marriage, adultery, separation, murder, war, prison, rambling, damnation, home, salvation, death, pride, humor, piety, rebellion, patriotism, larceny, determination, tragedy, rowdiness, heartbreak, and love. And Mother. And God. 'Rusty Cage' must fit in some of these categories."*
—liner notes, *Unchained*

BUOYED BY THE CRITICAL ACCLAIM AND the better-than-expected commercial success of *American Recordings*, Rubin and Cash were hot to widen their boundaries and expand their palettes on the next Cash offering, 1996's *Unchained*.

They started by choosing even more adventurous cover-song material, breaking down and reshaping a wide range of tunes until they came out of the kiln as Johnny Cash songs. That approach proved quite successful once again—but it wasn't without its hiccups. Most notably, the process of reinventing "Rusty Cage"—the spitfire, polyrhythmic grunge anthem from Soundgarden's 1991 album, *Badmotorfinger*—was almost nixed.

"When Rick first played it for me, I said no," Cash recalled. "I said, 'It's not for me, it's not my kind of thing.' But then they had the arrangement all put down to show me how I could do it, and it really worked. It starts off like a bluegrass thing, and I said, 'This is my cup of tea, I love this!'"[1]

The result is one of the most stirring tunes in the Cash latter-years canon. The first half of the track has Cash mirroring his sing-speak vocal with what's indeed a bluegrassy riff—but the second half of the song (a la the slowed-down section in Soundgarden's original) kicks in with drums and guitars blazing on a simply riveting groove. Cash sounds the part of a crazed caveman as he threatens to *break my rusty cage and run,*[2] nearly transgressing his low-register range with defiant cries and bellows.

No wonder Chris Cornell, former Soundgarden frontman and author of "Rusty Cage," was so effusive about Cash covering his material: "I got people calling me up and telling me, 'I heard the Johnny Cash version of 'Rusty Cage.' You write great lyrics!' At the time I thought, 'Why didn't you say that five years ago?' And I realized that when he sings a song you listen to what he has to say. And he draws from his own experience to make that song believable and get people to understand it. Johnny Cash is what a country like this needs, which is a soul … and in this day and age we really need more people like him, though I don't think there's ever gonna be anybody like him."[3]

Indeed, Rubin and Cash's genius stroke is their collective ability to choose a healthy mix of left-turn covers (aside from "Rusty Cage," Beck's "Rowboat" is another alt-rock gem, originally played in a country vein, but sounding more polished under the weight of Cash's voice), as well as traditional numbers. Believe it or not, among the most rousing, rollicking tunes on *Unchained* are spirited revamps of Hank Snow's version of "I've Been Everywhere," Don Gibson's version of "Sea Of Heartbreak," and Roy Clark's version of "I Never Picked Cotton"—all trad tunes that, with the Cash touch, sound just-conceived.

What's more, Jimmie Rodgers' version of the 1932 tune, "The One Rose," is fashioned with an authentic Delta blues feel, and the Carter Family-penned "Kneeling Drunkard's Plea" gets a hyped-up hillbilly treatment—as well as a Tom Petty harmony vocal.

Speaking of Petty, he and his Heartbreakers were Cash's de facto studio band for the *Unchained* sessions, and the Man in Black returned the favor by offering a world-weary, heartfelt rendition of "Southern Accents" for the final track listing. The presence of Petty and the Heartbreakers was no small deal, either—a full band represented another first for the Cash-Rubin conglomerate, ensuring that *Unchained* would indeed distance itself from *American Recordings*.

What a band it was. Petty and longtime cohorts Mike Campbell (guitar), Benmont Tench (keys), Howie Epstein (bass), and Steve Ferrone (drums) held down the fort. Guitarist Marty Stuart also played on half of the fourteen tracks, Flea—bassist for Red Hot Chili Peppers—played on "Spiritual," and Fleetwood Mac's Mick Fleetwood (drums) and Lindsey Buckingham (guitar) played on "Sea of Heartbreak."

"I was nervous about the record because I didn't know what direction we were going in,"[4] Cash noted. "When [Petty] found out I was starting a new album, he asked Rick if he could come by and play some on it. We hadn't even chosen musicians at that time. I think Tom was the first to volunteer to play on the album, and the other guys in the Heartbreakers came down after that.[5]

"I ran into Marty on a plane out West to the recording session and asked him to play, and with the first song, [a new version of Cash's '50s classic] 'Country Boy,' it felt great. We called the record *Unchained* because I felt so free to do whatever I wanted to, finally.[6]

"There was nothing binding us in the recording of this album. We had no major problems from anybody for any reason, and when we were all together it was like the songs flowed freely from all of the musicians through me, and the song became a part of me. We were all in accord."[7]

The reaction to *Unchained* from without the Cash-Rubin camp was decidedly positive. Whether it was Cash's outlaw persona that resonated with youth or not, something was working—especially with college-age kids and twentysomethings. Late in 1996, *Unchained* was the second most popular album on the playlists of the most influential college and noncommercial radio stations nationwide, noted *College Music Journal*. "He's won a new audience of young people who have a genuine respect for him, who admire him for his outsider persona," said James Lien, the journal's music editor.[8]

## FROM CASH'S OWN PEN ...

The mood on *American Recordings*, created via Cash and his

guitar only, is indeed charming—even compelling. On *Unchained,* however, Cash's prestigious studio band offered him an infinitely broader palette—a wide range of melodies and tempos to choose from. And more than a few of Cash's new tunes here simply rock the very essence of breakneck, barrelhouse roots and country, with blood and beer and saw-dust on the floor—along with a fair share of broken hearts and broken noses.

"Country Boy," noted previously, emerges as a brilliant, revved-up rockabilly number, complete with a Jerry Lee Lewis-styled piano breakdown. The track is so energetic and completely convincing that, when the awareness hits that the man singing the lyrics is a graying sixty-three-year-old, all you can do is wag your head from side to side.

Digging back through his archive once again, Cash summarily slays the original version of "Mean Eyed Cat" with a take he reveals as the true version. In the liner notes of *Unchained*—itself a treat full of inspired writing from Cash, as well as art-ful black-and-white photography—Cash said "Mean Eyed Cat" took him forty years to finish.

"I hadn't finished it in 1955 when, at a session, I sang the first two verses from Sam Phillips. He said, 'that's a keeper. I like that.' I said, 'But, it isn't finished.' He said it was good enough. I was totally surprised when it was released not long afterward. And all these years, every time I would see the title in print or hear the song on the radio, I'd cringe. Never once did I do the song on stage, and as the years passed, it bugged me more and more that the song was unfinished. So, about a year ago, I wrote the third verse. When I brought it to these sessions, it was like a new song … "[9]

Here "Mean Eyed Cat," an infectious toe-tapper about a spurned guy looking for his woman on the lam, showcases Cash's unparalleled storytelling ability. The meteoric backing track, in fact, is just about eclipsed by Cash's words and close-to-the-bone delivery.

Immediately following "Mean Eyed Cat" is the final Cash original on *Unchained,* a tribute to his long-departed brother Jack, "Meet Me in Heaven"—and as you might expect, the tempo is scaled way back, a chorus of gently picked acoustics and electrics forming the base while well-positioned organ flourishes add ecclesiastical believability: *We've seen the secret things revealed by God/ And we heard what the angels had to say/ Should you go first or if you follow me/ Will you meet me in heaven someday ...* [10]

"I always wanted to write a song called 'Meet Me in Heaven' because those words are on my brother's and my father's tombstones," Cash noted. "That song is one of those songs of peace that comes with my faith. That song was written to June, we've been together 34 years, and I think we're going to be together forever. I do believe in forever. That's what the song is all about, people who are going down a trail together forever."[11]

## "JESUS, I DON'T WANT TO DIE ALONE ... "

*Unchained*'s most telling testament to Cash's ability to make any song in the world his own is his show-stopping version of "Spiritual," written by alterative band Spain. And even though the words were penned by someone else (Josh Haden, son of jazz bassist Charlie Haden), nothing on *Unchained* comes close to conveying Cash's sense of quickening mortality and constant suffering. Toward the end of the dirge, Cash cuts loose, repeating his howling, primal need to God: *Jesus, oh Jesus/ All my troubles, all my pain ... It's gonna leave me once again.*[12] It's a deathbed prayer.

"Something has to be there to vex the spirit that enables you to deliver a song," Cash said later. "And on that day, it happened to be Flea [bassist for the Red Hot Chili Peppers]. He came by and wanted to play, but said he'd never played on a song like that one. But we did it in one take, exactly as you hear it on the record. There were tears in my eyes as I was singing it because I was overwhelmed with the feeling of everyone being in sync, all delivering this song together."[13]

A tangible sense of deep spirituality pervades *Unchained*, even more than on *American Recordings*. It's clear that Cash's health issues must have been hard reminders that his days were probably short—but what you get from Cash is not regret. Instead you get faith. You get resolve. You get a tenacious grip on life—as well as a never-say-die commitment to expressing himself in the light of God's presence. Wisdom and good humor fills Cash's spirit here.

## ANOTHER GRAMMY, ANOTHER MIDDLE FINGER

Not surprisingly, *Unchained* earned Cash his second consecutive Grammy for his work with Rubin (Best Country Album). But what generated even more press was an ad American Recordings placed in the March 14, 1998, issue of *Billboard*—just after the Grammy ceremonies took place. The ad was the famous photo of an incensed Cash flipping the bird to a photographer during his concert at San Quentin prison. The copy read, "American Recordings and Johnny Cash would like to acknowledge the Nashville music establishment and country radio for your support."

The crux of the issue was that Cash, a country music legend, wasn't getting airplay on country music stations—at least not the songs he'd recorded with Rick Rubin. During an on-air interview with WSMAM/FM Nashville, Cash offered that while he didn't pen the ad copy, it does express his sentiments regarding the exclusion of older artists on contemporary country stations. "I understand that people want to hear the new country," Cash said, "but when we lose our country music tradition—which is us old dinosaurs—then we've lost a lot."[14]

A number of other country music legends defended the Cash ad, reemphasizing that mature artists aren't being given a chance on radio.

"I think [Cash] probably did what 90 percent of the people in Nashville would like to do," famous fiddler Charlie Daniels said. "I think he just had enough guts to articulate it. Johnny is a legend. When these people who won't play him on the air—when the wind and the rain has washed the last vestiges of their names off their tombstones—somebody, somewhere, will still be listening to Johnny Cash. For radio to snub him, George Jones, and Merle Haggard is a travesty."[15]

Jones was more direct in his sentiments toward country music radio: "They ought to stick a wet squirrel in their mouth is what they ought to do … "[16]

CHAPTER SIXTEEN

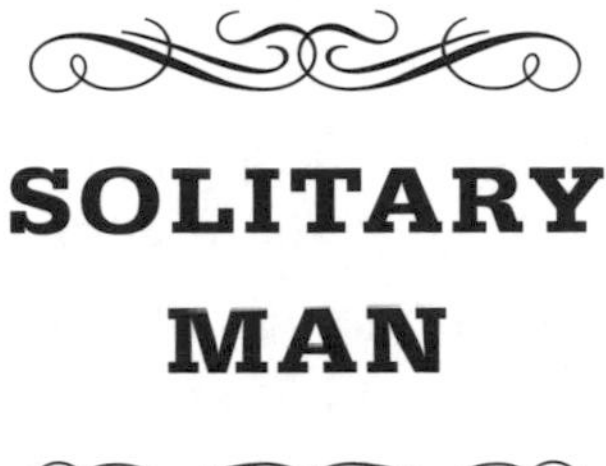

# SOLITARY MAN

BETWEEN THE RELEASE OF 1996'S UNCHAINED and 2000's *American III: Solitary Man*, Johnny Cash endured what was arguably the worst series of health crises in his life, a harrowing period rife with misdiagnoses, lengthy hospital stays, pneumonia, comas, and gut-wrenching moments when most everyone around Cash figured his number was up.

It began in October 1997 while Cash—supporting *Unchained* with a short tour—played a show in Flint, Michigan. At one point Cash leaned over to nab a wayward guitar pick, and he got dizzy and nearly fell down. Regaining his footing, Cash told the crowd matter-of-factly that he had Parkinson's disease. Some audience members, presumably thinking it was a joke, laughed. "It ain't funny," Cash replied. "[But] it's all right. I refuse to give it some ground in my life."[1]

Then in November, Cash was hit with double pneumonia and

drifted into a coma for almost two weeks. "I remember voices in the room," Cash told Larry King in November 2002. "I remember things they were saying. And I couldn't respond to [them] ... several times I wanted to wake up and tell them, 'I heard what you said, you know? I'm not dying!'"

Doctors at Nashville's Baptist Hospital, however, were sure Cash was a goner. But June Carter Cash put out the word on the Internet, asking fans around the world to pray for her husband on a predetermined evening.

On that very evening, Cash came around.

"They really thought they were gonna lose him—we all thought we were losing him," June later said. "He was in this coma—just down so far [that] there seemed to be no way to reach him—and I couldn't think of anything but to pray. So we prayed, and within a matter of hours, he just started squeezin' my hand."[2]

But Cash was a ways away from a clean bill of health. Besides temporarily losing the use of his legs due to the coma, doctors had a new diagnosis for Cash: Instead of Parkinson's, he was actually suffering from Shy-Drager syndrome, they said, an incurable, Parkinson's-like illness marked by neurological debilitation over time, then death. Upon hearing the news, Cash cancelled the rest of his tour—and, in fact, retired from touring altogether. Plus, the planned *Solitary Man* sessions were put indefinitely on hold while Cash recuperated in Jamaica and weighed his options.

Convalescence had little effect on Cash's famous spirit, however, as he repeatedly refused to name or discuss Shy-Drager, instead insisting that doctors had misdiagnosed him and that his health was actually improving.

"An old man knows in his bones if he's got a debilitating disease," he said. "And I knew I didn't have that one."[3]

For their part, doctors gave Cash meds, fully expecting Shy-Drager to do in Cash at any time.

But two years later, Cash's skeptical pronouncements proved correct. Not only was he not dead yet, he didn't have Shy-Drager, either. This veteran of two consecutive misdiagnoses was now suffering from diabetic neuropathy (later termed autonomic neuropathy), they said, a progressive disease of the nervous system. ("I'm not sure what that means," Cash said after his diagnosis, "except I think it means you're getting old and shaky.")[4] The keys for survival were now weaning himself off the Shy-Drager meds, steering clear of cold weather, and watching his diet.

Cash noted that his physician said, "If you had had [Shy-Drager] three years ago when it was diagnosed, you'd be dead. And you're getting better. So we'll forget about that disease." To which Cash replied, "Well, I knew I didn't have such a nasty-sounding disease anyway.[5]

"I feel good," he continued. "I take my walk every morning here in Jamaica. I play in the sunshine, ride around in my golf cart, and just get a lot of exercise. God was merciful to me and let me live. And I'm cherishing every year now and really enjoying life."[6]

## "I WON'T BACK DOWN"

Between further bouts with pneumonia, Cash had some time to choose and record tracks for what was the long-overdue third album in the Cash-Rubin canon, *Solitary Man*. Some days he only had enough energy to try a small handful of vocal takes, but that proved good enough as Rubin eventually emerged to begin formal sessions.

"I began this album as the last one, in the cabin, in the middle of a 50-acre compound surrounded by cedar trees, deer, goats, and peacocks," Cash wrote in the album liner notes. "The window unit air conditioner doesn't work anymore. We had buffalo, and every time it came on, they rammed it with their horns. Sometimes we have to stop tape for a thunderstorm. We play back the songs and the mockingbirds sing along with it."

*Solitary Man* is more stripped-down than *Unchained*, but carries more instrumental flourishes than *American Recordings*. No drums or bass guitars or electrics, mind you—simply acoustic instruments and the occasional keyboard flourish by Benmont Trench, landing *Solitary Man* squarely between Cash's two previous projects, sonically speaking. Cash noted in an interview that "one of the purposes of the album [was] to stretch as far as we could for a variety of themes and songs and beats and tunes, but to be sure that I could feel them personally, that they belonged to me when I did them."[7]

And while *Solitary Man* finds the Man in Black sounding decidedly older and weaker—something not apparent on *American Recordings* or *Unchained*—its opening tune, Cash's acoustic cover of "I Won't Back Down" by Tom Petty & the Heartbreakers, is wonderfully appropriate given his circumstances over the latter two years: *You can stand me up at the gates of hell/ But I won't back down/ Gonna stand my ground, won't be turned around/ And I'll keep this world from draggin' me down ...*[8]

Interestingly, Cash takes the road less traveled during this anthem of defiance, juxtaposing the war-cry lyrics with an eerie sense of feeble resignation, his voice quivering and wavering like a man who's preparing to back down. It's at once unnerving and inspiring—you want to pat Cash on the back for this gutsy stance ... and you want to clear away before his tower of strength comes crumbling down.

The title track—one of Neil Diamond's many hits—is a seemingly odd selection, given that it doesn't exactly hug the cutting edge. But as Diamond was a guest on Cash's coast-to-coast network variety show (he dueted "Where the Old Red River Flows" with Cash on February 11, 1970), the association and allegiance becomes more understandable. In addition, the lyrics of "Solitary Man" certainly reflect Cash's loner persona, especially his unwavering commitment to rugged individualism.

## "WAYFARING STRANGER"

*Solitary Man* also finds Cash even more in touch with his soul and approaching mortality than ever. Cash returns U2's favor (read: "The Wanderer") by covering a quick-tempoed take of the now-classic track from *Achtung Baby*, "One." Backed by acoustics, a sparse piano, and a dirge-like organ, Cash—as is becoming his unparalleled artistic trademark—makes the U2 tune sound like a brand new song, coloring it with the sense of love shared between a lifelong couple nearing the end of their days. And "Before My Time," one of four Cash originals on *Solitary Man,* speaks tenderly and longingly about the unassailable passing of time.

In addition, Cash unearths a quiet, bluesy old tune he once sang to fellow grammar school students—"That Lucky Old Sun (Just Rolls Around Heaven All Day)"—and won a five-dollar prize in the process. The lyrics reflect Psalm-centric themes: *Oh, Lord above, can't you hear ... me cryin'/ Tears rollin' down my eyes ... / Take me ... to paradise/ Show me that river, take me across/ Wash all my troubles away ...*[9] In Cash's hands, "That Lucky Old Sun" is a sustained prayer, a lonesome cry of the human condition.

Perhaps the most stirring song on *Solitary Man* is Cash's version of "The Mercy Seat." Originally penned by Nick Cave and Mick Harvey, this gut-wrenching selection is composed from the perspective of a death-row inmate—who insists he's innocent—about to sit in an electric chair: *And the mercy seat is waiting/ And I think my head is burning/ And in a way I'm yearning to be done with all this weighing of the truth/ An eye for an eye and a tooth for a tooth/ And anyway I told the truth/ And I'm not afraid to die ...*[10]

The lethal combination of Cash's woeful baritone, Tench's left-field piano running straight outta Liberace land juxtaposed with mournful organ lines, and the crestfallen, almost overwhelming words—filled to the gills with Christian/biblical imagery—makes "The Mercy Seat" one of Cash's most important musical statements. It's Cash at his most potent, reflective, and empathetic. (And it's only in listening to the goth-laden original, complete with unintelligible lyrics, that you realize the Man in Black has created yet another living, breathing entity—a beautiful, disturbing, God-honoring musical piece of social conscience and spiritual reckoning.)

"When I heard that song, I'd just been seeing the news the day before about executions in Texas," Cash recalled. "And Tennessee had executed a man. I don't have a stand on capital punishment. I won't say one way or another, because my heart is with the victims. The song, I don't feel like it's an indictment on capital punishment. I think it's something that we should call our attention to. If a man's been there 25 years, maybe we should consider whether or not he has become a good human being and do we still want to kill him."[11]

"Mary of the Wild Moor"—a tragic mountain ballad about a young mother who dies protecting her baby from a snowstorm—is a song Cash had wanted to record for years. "I was probably 3 years old when I heard that the first time, and I always knew someday I would record it. I guess I must have thought about it at every session I ever had, and, finally, I just went ahead and did it."[12]

(While there are no obvious spiritual references in the latter song, there is an interesting connection to Bob Dylan, who sang "Mary of the Wild Moor" in a November 1980 concert shortly after his conversion to Christianity: "This is a real old song. I used to sing this before I even wrote any songs. Last time we played it—I think it was in Tucson—there was a review in the newspaper that I'd like to get straight. The man who … reviewed it … said [it] was about Jesus being born in the manger; well, that's not entirely true about this song … it's just an old southern mountain ballad, that's all there is, about someone dying in the snowstorm.")[13]

*Solitary Man*—touted by many at the time of its release as

perhaps Cash's last album—ends appropriately enough with the dour-yet-comforting "Wayfaring Stranger," a song that was passed around the Appalachian mountains for generations by word of mouth. In this minor-key dirge—beautifully enhanced by fiddle, accordion, and piano—Cash deftly brings all of his pain, faith, and heavenly desire to the old spiritual. In the end, it becomes Cash's personal eulogy:

*I am a poor wayfaring stranger*
*Wandering through this world of woe*
*But there's no sorrow, toil, or danger*
*In that bright land to which I go*

*I'm going there to see my father*
*I'm going there no more to roam*
*I'm just a going over Jordan*
*I'm only going over home*

*I know dark clouds will gather 'round me*
*I know my way is rough and steep*
*But golden fields lie out before me*
*Where all the saints their vigils keep*

*I'm going there to see my mother*
*I'm going there no more to roam*
*I'm just a going over Jordan*
*I'm only going over home*

*I'm going there to see my Savior*
*To sing His praise forevermore*
*I'm just a going over Jordan*
*I'm only going over home*

"The Master of Life's been good to me. He gives me good

health now and helps me to continue doing what I love. He has given me strength to face past illnesses, and victory in the face of defeat. He has given me life and joy where others saw oblivion. He has given new purposes to live for. New services to render and old wounds to heal. Life and love go on. Let the music play."[14]

CHAPTER SEVENTEEN

# THE MAN COMES AROUND

AFTER JOHNNY CASH CUT HIS LAST vocal for *Solitary Man,* another three years would pass before the public got another taste of the Cash-Rubin studio magic. But even though Cash promised his follow-up would be "the best I've ever done,"[1] others weren't sure he'd even live long enough to record again.[2] Indeed, months and months went by, then a year, then two … and even fair-minded folks weren't convinced a new album was imminent.

There were some understandable reasons for the delay—namely Cash's health. To put it bluntly, the Man in Black was aging—and fast.

Pneumonia nearly killed him in early 2001.[3] His once thick, black-gray mane was now a whispy, snowy white. He had difficulty getting around—a wheelchair would soon be his regular companion. His feet and hands swelled like balloons most of the time. His energy and immune system were at rock-bottom levels. Glaucoma clouded his eyes to such a degree that he required a magnifying glass to read chord charts and lyric sheets—forget his beloved books on early Roman and Christian history.

What's more, a dentist had broken Cash's jaw and failed to properly reset it. His options were surgery (which could have ended his singing career if anything went wrong) or pain meds (which surely would have resurrected his addictive tendencies). So Cash chose a third option—pain. "He told me the only time he didn't feel pain was when he was onstage," author Charles Hirshberg said.[4]

This is what Cash faced when he finally tackled sessions for *American IV: The Man Comes Around*. Again Cash could only record vocals in short segments lest he run out of breath, his seriously diminished lung capacity evident in what used to be an earth-shaking baritone.[5]

"I had some nightmare days in the studio," Cash admitted. "I didn't have any voice or lung power left. I'd have a studio full of musicians and all this expense goin', and I couldn't sing a drop. It wasn't just the money; it was the very idea of not being able to sing. That was the thing that really hurt.[6]

But Cash once again bulldozed through these obstacles. "I found strength to work on this album just to spite the disease," he continued. "I could've stayed at home and pouted in my room and turned the lights down low and got real mournful and sad and cried in my beer or whatever, my milk, whatever I was drinking ... but I didn't let that happen. I came in and opened up my mouth and tried to let something come out a few times. As it turns out, there are tracks on this album that I recorded when it was the last thing in the world I thought I'd be able to do. And those are the ones that have the feeling, the passion, the fire, the fervor."[7]

## NO PAIN, NO GAIN

Apparently the extra time and sweat was worth it. *The Man Comes Around* was released in November 2002, and it captured the collective imagination of music aficionados, critics, and industry insiders like nothing Cash had heretofore created.

"[It] represents some of Cash's best work, material on par with his seminal Sun recordings and the career-defining Folsom Prison and San Quentin live albums," one critic wrote. "*American III: Solitary Man* from 2000 sounded tentative, as if Cash's poor health had managed to steal a bit of his fire. *The Man Comes Around* redeems Cash, though; these songs tell a story of mortal frailty, the desire for reconciliation, and the indomitable human spirit.[8]

"Parts of his fourth collaboration with producer Rick Rubin are, quite simply, stunning. The high points are among the highest of Cash's legendary career ... even the throwaway moments are often more gripping than many artists can ever hope to achieve."[9]

Admittedly the tone of *The Man Comes Around* is even more reflective and, yes, dismal than the feel of *Solitary Man*, which itself plays like a swan song. This issue wasn't lost on Cash: "At one point I said to Rick, 'we're really getting sad and mournful with this album.' And he said, 'Not depression-sad, just sad for the sake of sadness.' After that, I thought, 'you know, if that's what's coming, let's go for it.'"[10]

Still, there was no denying it. From now on, whenever Cash set foot in the recording studio, everyone (including Cash) knew it could be his last moment behind the mic. *Solitary Man* was supposed to be the end. But Cash beat the odds and came back with *The Man Comes Around*—and if it was to be his finale, the fifteen-track monster fit the bill.

On the whole, the album is again defined by earthy, acoustic instruments, a bevy of superstar guest musicians and vocalists, and Cash's weary, wisdom-filled, earth-moving vocals tearing into cover songs like he's the one who conjured them out of thin air. Nothing new here—the other three CDs in the celebrated Cash-Rubin cadre are similar in that respect. It's just that with *The Man Comes Around,* Cash approaches his tunes like he's made sweet peace with God and is laughing in the face of death; there's an overriding sense of rising above evident all over the place.

## "A WHIRLWIND IN THE THORN TREE"

The title track (and opener) is immediately arresting because a crackly recording of Cash quoting from the Book of Revelation precedes his actual launch into the foot-stomping ditty. But the tune itself does center around a triumphant description of Christ's return: *There's a man goin' 'round takin' names/ And he decides who to free and who to blame/ Everybody won't be treated all the same/ There'll be a golden ladder reaching down/ When the man comes around.*[11] Unabashedly fire and brimstone theologically speaking, Cash nevertheless conveys a convincingly happy tone via simple, major chords and an upbeat tempo.

Cash reveals in the album liner notes that the idea for the track came to him while he was traveling in England—like the Mexican horns in "Ring of Fire" coming to him during a dream. In it, Cash walks into Buckingham Palace and Queen Elizabeth looks at him and says, "Johnny Cash! You're like a thorn tree in a whirlwind." Then Cash woke up.

Soon Cash was devouring large chunks of the Bible once again, leaning heavily on Job and Revelation, and it took him almost half a year to get the song right. (Interestingly, the Bible typically characterizes whirlwinds as a sweeping, destructive force that overtakes the wicked—and thorns are typically the emblem of the wicked.)

"I've wanted to write a spiritual that would be worthy of recording," Cash said. "I worked really hard on this song … I finally realized where I was going with it—kind of a spiritual odyssey of the apocalypse."[12]

Guitarist (and ex-son in law) Marty Stuart characterized the track as the "most strangely marvelous, wonderful, gothic, mysterious, Christian thing that only God and Johnny Cash could create together."[13]

## "HURT" AND EVERYTHING AFTER

If "The Man Comes Around" isn't a powerful enough musical statement, the song that follows it immediately threw listeners over the edge. Cash's cover of "Hurt"—from the Nine Inch Nails' library of gloom—was among the most talked about tunes of 2003 and is certainly Cash's best cover song rendition in his entire career. The sense of loss and regret Cash wrings from Trent Reznor's drug-addled lyrics is devastating and infinitely saddening—not to mention the accompaniment that moves from soft acoustic guitar to pounding piano and mournful strings, which augment the desperation and resignation in Cash's voice. (Eventually Cash would make a video for "Hurt" that impacted the entire music industry in 2003—and beyond.)

While Reznor gets kudos for writing amazing melodies and words, Cash flat out immortalizes "Hurt." A century from now, Cash's version will stand as the definitive interpretation. Cash's feeble vocal conveys humility and brokenness; conversely, Reznor's vocal (in the original version) conveys angst and depression—all demonstrating the vast difference between a twentysomething and seventysomething performer.

But just as with the "Rusty Cage" dilemma, "Hurt" almost didn't make it to tape. At first Rubin didn't want to present the tune to Cash because of song's sole cuss word, which appears in the line, "I wear this crown of sh--." He wound up substituting the word "thorns," instead. And when Rubin first played "Hurt" for Cash, it was the melody itself that didn't turn Cash's crank.

"When I heard the record, I said, 'I can't do that song,'" Cash recalled. "'It's not my style.' [Rick] said, 'Well, let's try it another way.' He put down a track and I listened to it ... From there we started working on it until we got the record made."[14]

Other interesting cover choices—most all of them connected as well in off-kilter ways to the theme of mortality—include Simon & Garfunkel's "Bridge Over Troubled Water," which leaves Cash sounding like a man who wishes he could have done more for others; a pretty faithful rendition of The Beatles' "In My Life" becomes Cash's magical testament to friends and lovers; the traditional "Danny Boy" (with church pipe organ) is even more dirge-like in its treatment here—no surprise ... it was recorded in an Episcopal church; "First Time I Ever Saw Your Face"—yes, the AM radio staple Roberta Flack made famous in the '70s—becomes, through Cash's vocal chords, a teary-eyed look back on a life of loving the same person; on the Eagles' "Desperado," Cash sounds like an aging outlaw itching to exit this world in blaze of glory; his duet with Nick Cave on Hank Williams' "I'm So Lonesome I Could Cry" is bleak but somehow peaceful; and the closer, "We'll Meet Again," feels like Cash's goodbye to us all—a clarinet lends a flamboyant, French Quarter-funeral flair.

The decision to cover Depeche Mode's "Personal Jesus," while a gutsy move by Cash, feels a little out of place. Still his brilliant delivery about the con-artistry of those who solicit faith in God just like slick salesmen or auctioneers is quite evident.

"That's probably the most evangelical gospel song I've ever recorded," Cash later said of "Personal Jesus." "I don't know that the writer meant it to be that, but that's what it is."[15]

Right up there with "Hurt" in terms of breaking new ground with cover material is Cash's version of Sting's "I Hung My Head." The yarn about bad luck and an accidental murder takes on stark, deeper meaning as Cash embodies the protagonist's sense of guilt, shame, and penance. What's more, Cash deals yet again with the inevitability of death—and does so with comfortable authority.[16]

## "LIKE FRANK SINATRA, ELVIS PRESLEY ... "

Beyond its many superlatives, *The Man Comes Around* proves once again that Cash is a master of song interpretation—he never fails to make each cover tune he touches ring out like one of his originals. "Like Frank Sinatra, Elvis Presley, and other prolific giants in American music, Mr. Cash's capacity to transform disparate material—in his case country, folk, gospel, and rock 'n' roll—into its own unique language is as commanding as ever."[17]

Another critic notes, "Johnny Cash doesn't sing songs. He inhabits them … when Cash sings them, he owns them. They become colors in a larger mosaic or maybe a wall-sized mural depicting the constant flip-flopping between truth and deceit, light and darkness, honor and disgrace, and good and evil that constitutes our earthly tenure. Like Picasso's 'Guernica,' they're a depiction of terrible beauty. It's all about that inescapable duality. And Cash is here to tell you that, what God has joined, let no man tear asunder."[18]

## "IT'S BEEN FUN"

Apparently Cash wasn't pleased with some of his vocals by the time *The Man Comes Around* was in the can, and he worried that perhaps Rubin may have grown weary of him. (Plus, while the Cash-Rubin combo earned a handful of Grammys, none of them to this point sold a ton—at least not in comparison to other groups Rubin's produced, such as Red Hot Chili Peppers.)

"I had just finished my last vocal for the record," Cash

recalled, "and I shook hands with Rick, and I said, 'It's been fun.' I think it was my way of saying I understand if he wanted to call it quits."

Cash, as you might expect, had little to worry about.

"He immediately asked what I wanted to do next. I mentioned the black gospel album, and then I mentioned an album of songs that would show my musical roots, and Rick said, 'Let's do them both.' I was dumbfounded. It was just what I wanted to hear. I had thought I might be finally at the point where I would only be singing for myself."[19]

Later Cash announced that he had indeed launched work on a black gospel album slated to include his gag cuts from the likes of the Golden Gate Quartet and the Five Blind Boys of Alabama. Following this project, Cash noted that he'd probably attempt an album that would survey folk and country songs extended "all the way back to Stephen Foster."

Asked if retirement may finally be a possibility instead, Cash snapped back, "No, no, no no, no. I'd die if I retire. Like a shark—got to keep moving."[20]

CHAPTER EIGHTEEN

# HURT

MERE DAYS AFTER THE MAN COMES *Around* was released, it was obvious that Johnny Cash had created what was arguably the most potent, revealing musical statement of his entire career—the praise surrounding the album was that intense.

But no one was prepared for what happened next.

Silver-screen artiste Mark Romanek (director of Robin Williams' acclaimed *One Hour Photo*) got together with Cash to make a music video for his version of "Hurt," the haunting song originally written by Nine Inch Nails' Trent Reznor.

"I begged Rick Rubin to let me shoot something to that track," said Romanek, who got an earful of *The Man Comes Around* a few months before its release date and became enamored with Cash's rendition of "Hurt."

It wasn't an open-and-shut deal for Romanek, a friend of Rubin's and a longtime fan of the Man in Black. (Romanek was so hot after the gig that he offered to shoot the video for free.) Eventually the arm-twisting worked—but almost as quickly his plans to film "Hurt" in Los Angeles came crashing down in the wake of Cash's unpredictable health. Worse still, Cash had no intentions of sticking around Tennessee in cold weather—he was headed to Jamaica for a long respite. Romanek had only a few days remaining to do … something. It would take a complete reinvention of everything he conceived the video to be, but he wasn't about to stop now—so he hopped a red-eye to Nashville.[1]

The next day Romanek scouted locations for the shoot inside Cash's house and at his museum, The House of Cash. "It had been closed for a long time," the director said. "The place was in such a state of dereliction. That's when I got the idea that maybe we could be extremely candid about the state of Johnny's health—as candid as Johnny has always been in his songs."[2]

The ideas were coming quickly—but they didn't resemble anything close to the glamorous innovation Romanek used, for example, on Michael and Janet Jackson's "Scream" clip. Nope, the "Hurt" video will show the aged Cash plainly, with no gimmicks or camera trickery.

Half of Romenek's live shots of Cash singing the words to "Hurt" were captured at Cash's house, with June in a few frames watching him sadly from a staircase landing; the other half took place in the House of Cash, first with Johnny seated at an upright piano, then at a lavish dinner table loaded up with goblets, champagne, caviar, lobster, and exotic fruit … but no guests. The most stunning shots were of Cash himself, a fragile shell of his former robust self, his face and body wrecked by years of drugs and disease—and absolutely no attempts are made to disguise his galloping mortality.

The powerful live shots were then juxtaposed with archival footage of a younger, healthier Cash in different venues in different years—at San Quentin prison, hopping a railroad car, strumming his six-string on TV, riding a tour bus with June, visiting his abandoned childhood home in Dyess, John Carter coming home after his birth, and several frames of Cash in Israel during the filming of *Gospel Road*. (The intercut shots were from Cash's private collection and lent to Romanek, who spent weeks sweating through hundreds of hours of videotape.)

The result, according to *Rolling Stone*, is "one of the most intense and affecting videos in memory."[3] An MTV scribe proclaimed, "In the short history of music videos, few have had the emotional heft and visual impact of the clip shot by director Mark Romanek in the Tennessee home of the ailing country legend."[4]

Though interpretations are numerous, "Hurt" seems to hit viewers at specific primal points of interest, namely: mortality and the fleeting passage of time—indeed how truly everything and everyone we know eventually "goes away in the end."

"This [concept] is completely and utterly alien to what videos are supposed to be," Romanek said. "Videos are supposed to be eye candy—hip and cool and all about youth and energy. This one is about someone [moving] toward the twilight of his career, this powerful, legendary figure who is dealing with issues and emotions you're not used to encountering in videos … [5] I think it really sucker-punches people in that way."[6]

Rick Rubin said the video is now a historical document. "I cried the first time I saw it,"[7] he said. "If you were moved to that kind of emotion in the course of a two-hour movie, it would be a great accomplishment. To do it in a four-minute music video is shocking.[8]

"I spoke to Bono and he compared what Johnny is doing now to what Elvis Presley did in the 1950s. Then Elvis represented a new youth culture, and it shocked and terrified everyone because culture wasn't about youth before him. Now we live in a youth culture, and Johnny Cash is showing the experience of a much older generation. It's just as radical."[9]

Rubin sent a copy of the "Hurt" video to Trent Reznor, the song's author.

"We were in the studio, getting ready to work—and I popped it in," Reznor says. "By the end I was really on the verge of tears. I'm working with [former Rage Against the Machine vocalist] Zach de la Rocha, and I told him to take a look. At the end of it, there was just dead silence. There was, like, this moist clearing of our throats and then, 'Uh, okay, let's get some coffee.'"[10]

Romanek said he created "Hurt" with no ambitious aspirations, fully expecting that it may rise to the level of an artsy clip—and definitely wouldn't get much of a reception at MTV or VH1. (Soon it would be rotating regularly on VH1 and MTV2 and later blowing more minds by nabbing a whopping six Video Music Award nominations from MTV, including Video of the Year—Cash is the oldest nominee ever.)

"If you watch what's on MTV, you don't see anything like this," Rubin added. "You won't see anything from any artist in

Johnny's age range, and you won't see anything with this kind of serious content. It really sticks out like a sore thumb."[11]

Cash was also taken aback when he first saw the video, Rubin said. And it was only because of his family's encouragement that he agreed to let it be released.[12]

"I think 'Hurt' is the best anti-drug song I ever heard. If it doesn't scare you away from taking drugs, nothing will," said Cash, who has battled and overcome addictions to pills and booze. "I never did the needle, but I did everything else."[13]

"I'm most proud of the fact that it's causing this visceral, emotional reaction," Romanek said. "That's the whole reason to make any sort of film. You don't often have the opportunity to do that with a music video because that's not usually what you're being asked to accomplish."[14]

## AFTER "HURT"

Rosanne Cash was none too excited to watch the "Hurt" video at first, but during a visit to her dad and stepmom's place, Johnny asked her if she'd seen it. Nope. "I watched it with him and June, and I was weeping and weeping through the whole thing," she said. "My dad was completely clear-eyed and focused on the merits of the video, which is so much like him. He's able to focus on the most awful truths with an artist's eye."[15]

"I don't especially like making videos," Cash told MTV News' Kurt Loder. "It's just work. Sometimes it's really fun and I enjoy it very much, but the getting there and all that usually just isn't.

"I enjoyed doing the 'Hurt' video because I felt we were doing something worthwhile, that it was something kind of special...I was there right in the middle of the thing. So after it was put together, I watched with a critical eye to see what I could find wrong with it. And I didn't find much wrong with it.

"I didn't get any direct criticism about 'Hurt,'" he explained. "I didn't get any preachers calling me or anything like that. People who I expected to not like it let me know that they turned a deaf ear to it. It would be all right as long as I didn't play that video for them. Ninety-eight percent of them were complimentary; I didn't get very much flack at all. My children, my grandchildren, they all love it."[16]

Romanek repeatedly noted that the Cash we see in the video is far less gloomy in real life. And especially to his friends and loved ones, he was total cut-up.

In fact, when Romanek asked June if she would appear briefly in the video, Cash deadpanned, "Yeah, honey, why don't you dance naked on the piano here while I'm playing?" The room roared.[17]

CHAPTER NINETEEN

# EVERYONE I KNOW GOES AWAY IN THE END

DEATH WAS NEVER FAR FROM JOHNNY Cash throughout his musical career. But despite close calls involving everything from car accidents to forest fires, drug addiction, drug overdoses, heart disease, pneumonia, diabetes, comas, or nervous system problems, Cash never failed to escape death's clutches.

Many people who Cash loved dearly, however, weren't so fortunate—his big brother Jack (d. 1944), his guitarist Luther Perkins (d. 1968), his father-in-law Ezra J. Carter (d. 1975), his mother-in-law, Maybelle Carter (d. 1978), his daddy Ray Cash (d. 1985), singer Roy Orbison (d. 1988), his momma Carrie Rivers Cash (d. 1991), singer Carl Perkins (d. 1998), and his sister-in-law Anita Carter (d. 1999), to name a few.

But the years 2002 and 2003 proved to be particularly painful ones for the Man in Black: In the space of eighteen months, Cash—who was also nearing the end of his days—would lose four loved ones to death's clutches.

## WAYLON JENNINGS—FEBRUARY 12, 2002

Jennings was a leader of country music's "outlaw" movement in the 1970s, released more than eighty hit singles, and logged studio and road time with Cash's country music supergroup, the Highwaymen, along with Willie Nelson and Kris Kristofferson. Jennings died in his sleep, peacefully, in Arizona after a long bout with diabetes that saw his foot amputated. He was sixty-four.

"Losing Waylon was a tough one," Cash told Larry King in a November 2002 televised interview. "We were very close. We were very good friends."

Jennings escaped death's grasp in dramatic fashion very early in his career, when he gave up his airplane seat to rockabilly star J.P. Richardson, "The Big Bopper." That flight also included superstar performers Buddy Holly and Ritchie Valens—and crashed, killing everyone aboard, on February 3, 1959 (a.k.a., the Day the Music Died).

Jennings was known for doing things his way—much like Cash, who roomed, drugged, and picked with Jennings early in their careers.

Among his most famous tunes (along with those he dueted with Willie Nelson) are "Are You Sure Hank Done It That Way?" "I'm a Ramblin' Man," "Mammas Don't Let Your Babies Grow Up to Be Cowboys," and the theme from *The Dukes of Hazzard* TV series, which he also narrated.[1]

## HOWIE EPSTEIN—FEBRUARY 23, 2003

Epstein, a bassist and former member of Tom Petty & the Heartbreakers, died of a suspected drug overdose in Sante Fe, New Mexico. He was forty-seven.

Epstein was a lauded musician and producer for more than two decades. Besides his work with the Heartbreakers, Epstein played on a few Bob Dylan albums in the 1980s, worked with Roy Orbison, Del Shannon, John Hiatt, and Stevie Nicks, and produced a Grammy-award winning album (*The Lost Years*) for John Prine.

Cash employed Epstein as the "house" bassist for his 1996 album, *Unchained*. Not coincidentally, Epstein was also the longtime boyfriend of Cash's stepdaughter, singer Carlene Carter. In fact, Epstein produced two of her albums—and one nabbed a Grammy nomination.

"I'm devastated," Carter said. "I loved him very much. My kids thought of Howie as their father. We had a good life together for 15 years. We've been apart since May last year, and all I know is I'm going to miss him very much."[2]

## SAM PHILLIPS—JULY 30, 2003

The man who told Cash to "come on in!" before the world heard a blip of his music died after a lengthy illness in Memphis, Tennessee. He was eighty.

The pioneering Phillips founded Sun Records, cut Elvis Presley's first record, and also signed the likes of Cash, Carl Perkins, Jerry Lee Lewis, Roy Orbison, Charlie Rich, and Jackie Brenston—basically delivering newborn rock 'n' roll to a hungry public.

The latter artist, while not a household name, is considered by many experts, historians, and critics to be the author of the very first rock 'n' roll record ever, "Rocket 88," recorded in 1951. Phillips' shadow was long and broad, indeed.

"He meant everything," said Howard Kramer, curatorial director of the Rock and Roll Hall of Fame and Museum. "Without Sam Phillips, the landscape of contemporary music would be completely different."

Like Cash and Presley, Phillips is a member of the Rock and Roll Hall of Fame (original inductee, 1986) as well as the Country Music Hall of Fame (2001).[3]

## JUNE CARTER CASH—MAY 15, 2003

June was admitted to Nashville's Baptist Hospital for surgery to repair a heart valve, and she died due to complications. She was seventy-three. Her death was shocking to many; especially since she went before Johnny.

Cash was amazed at her strength, even to very end. "She told me in the hospital, 'Don't worry about me ... go to work.' Three days after the funeral—everybody said, 'You're crazy,' but three days after the funeral, I was in the studio. And I stayed in the studio for two weeks."[4]

At June's funeral at the First Baptist Church of Hendersonville, stepdaughter Rosanne Cash gave the eulogy—quite a statement as June wasn't Rosanne's mother by birth.

"The relationship between stepmother and children is by definition complicated," Rosanne said. "But June eliminated the confusion by banning the words stepchild and stepmother from her vocabulary, and from ours. When she married my father in 1968, she brought with her two daughters, Carlene and Rosey. My dad brought with him four daughters: Kathy, Cindy, Tara, and me. Together they had a son, John Carter. But she always said, 'I have seven children.' She was unequivocal about it.

"In her eyes, there were two kinds of people in the world:

those she knew and loved, and those she didn't know and loved. She looked for the best in everyone; it was a way of life for her. If you pointed out that a particular person was perhaps not totally deserving of her love, and might in fact be somewhat of a lout, she would say, 'Well, honey, we just have to lift him up.' She was forever lifting people up. It took me a long time to understand that what she did when she lifted you up was to mirror the very best parts of you back to yourself. She was like a spiritual detective: she saw into all your dark corners and deep recesses, saw your potential and your possible future, and the gifts you didn't even know you possessed, and she 'lifted them up' for you to see. She did it for all of us, daily, continuously.

"But her great mission and passion were lifting up my dad. If being a wife were a corporation, June would have been the CEO. It was her most treasured role. She began every day by saying, 'What can I do for YOU, John?' Her love filled up every room he was in, lightened every path he walked, and her devotion created a sacred, exhilarating place for them to live out their married life. My daddy has lost his dearest companion, his musical counterpart, his soul mate, and best friend."[5]

## "FOR FIVE MINUTES WITH JUNE ..."

"When my wife died, I booked myself into the studio just to work, to occupy myself so I would be doing something, and I found that that's the thing I really wanted to do, to be in the studio," Cash told *Time* magazine. "That's what I been doing. That's what I'm gonna be doing for a while."[6]

In June, Cash traveled to Maces Springs, Virginia, for a Carter Family Fold country music festival—an event he and June attended often. Though he was weak and not in the best voice, Cash sang and spoke to the crowd: "I don't know hardly what to say tonight about being up here without her," Cash said somberly. "The pain is so severe there is no way of describing it."[7]

"He tried to contain himself," said the Reverend Courtney Wilson of First Baptist Church, "but her passing took his last spark, the last bit of his heart."[8]

"One day there was just the two of us sitting there," former son-in-law Marty Stuart recalled, "and he broke down and started crying and said, 'Man, I miss her so bad.' I didn't know what to say, so I held his hand. He loved my wife Connie, who's been a friend to that family for a long time. He grabbed my hand and said, 'Son, cling to her; cling to her; cling to her.' What I saw at that moment is that he would have traded every bit of fame, fortune—everything that Johnny Cash meant to the world—for five minutes with June."[9]

## "THERE'S NO CURE FOR LIFE, EITHER"

When Larry King asked Cash if there was any cure for his diagnosis of autonomic neuropathy, he offered a typically Cash-ian deadpan reply: "No, I don't think so. But that's all right. There's no cure for life, either."

Indeed Cash poured his days into recording after June died, but as happens with many long-married couples, when the husband or wife dies, the surviving spouse often doesn't survive for long, either.

He said as much to MTV's Kurt Loder, who conducted Cash's final videotaped interview, just weeks before his death. "Oh, I expect my life to end pretty soon," Cash said resolutely. "You know, I'm 71 years old. I have great faith, though. I have unshakeable faith."[10]

“I just don’t have any fear of death,” Cash wrote in his autobiography. “I haven’t lost a minute’s sleep over it. I’m very much at peace with myself and with my God. I accept this disease because it’s the will of God; it’s Him working in my life. And when He sees fit to take me from this world, I’ll be reunited with some good people I haven’t seen for a while.”[11]

Cash was admitted to Nashville’s Baptist Hospital a week before MTV’s Video Music Awards for a stomach ailment and was discharged on September 9.

After some resting at home, Cash’s plan was to head back into the studio with Rick Rubin to select songs for *American V*, for which fifty songs were already in the can.

But later that week, Cash was readmitted to the hospital—and his plans changed.

“He was aware things were closing down for him, and he was at peace,” said Rev. Wilson, who visited Cash in the hospital “He was ready to go home to God.”[12]

“That great light is a light that now leads me on and directs me and guides me,” Cash said during a recent CMT network interview. “That great light is the light of this world. That great light is the light out of this world, and into that better world. And I’m lookin’ forward to walkin’ into it with that great light.”

Welcome home, Johnny.

# TRIBUTES

**BILLY GRAHAM:** "One entertainment personality whose friendship Ruth and I have particularly valued is country music singer Johnny Cash, along with his wife, June Carter Cash. Johnny has won just about every award in his field, and his distinctive voice is loved by millions around the world. Some years ago, Johnny and June began coming to our Crusades to sing, and their presence and witness to Christ have drawn countless people to meetings who might not otherwise have come. We have laughed together and cried together as families, sharing each other's burdens during times of illness and heartache. We've been guests in each other's homes on many occasions and vacationed together from time to time. We have no better friends than Johnny and June."[1]

**TOM MORELLO** [guitarist, Rage Against the Machine, Audioslave]: "I was never a fan of country and western music, and then in, like, 1994, Rage Against the Machine were playing some European festivals, and I noticed that on one of the side stages Johnny Cash was playing. So I thought ... I'd go and check it out. I had heard that name from my youth, though I had never been a fan. I walked into this tent, and it was filled with thousands of people, and he was wearing a black suit, and it was absolutely one of the most mesmerizing hours of music I had ever seen in my entire life. The songs had such depth and gravity and power. He was such a charismatic person as well as a performer that I stood there hypnotized by this man and his music. Even though the genre was something that I could've cared less about, it was him as a performer that was totally compelling, and I became a fan and went out and got a lot of Johnny Cash records after that."[2]

**BONO**: "Nothing is as macho as Johnny Cash's voice. A real threat you will not find in a 22-year-old. You just won't. You can dress him up in leather pants, you can have him throw his TV out the hotel window. He can roar in front of all manner of white noise, but there's no real threat when you're a teenager, when you're in your 20s or when you're [in your] 30s. The real sh--, or what they say in New Orleans, the other kind of sh--, comes from the perspective of being in the trenches and having been around a while. All the blues guys had it. Muddy Waters, John Lee Hooker, B.B. King. Johnny Cash has that and the voice of authority for me."[3]

**KIRK HAMMETT** [lead guitarist, Metallica]: "He was one of the originals. He was one of the first guys to embody that 'Don't mess with me' image. With Johnny Cash, what you saw is what you got. And then you got a heavy dose of reality with it."[4]

**JAMES HETFIELD** [vocalist-guitarist, Metallica]: "He's speaking for the broken people—people who can't speak up or no one wants to hear. And when you hear, 'Hi, I'm Johnny Cash,' that's all you need. It's him and his guitar speaking from the heart, in black, not flashy, not anything. He's just there putting his heart out through his music."[5]

**ANTHONY KIEDIS** [vocalist, Red Hot Chili Peppers]: "Johnny Cash is an icon and a legend and just a bold reality. And he comes from a million years ago, and he'll live on for a million more years. He makes music that comes from an incredibly deep and powerful place."[6]

**PHARRELL WILLIAMS** [the Neptunes]: "I don't think there's a rap artist that has more songs about killing somebody than Johnny Cash does."[7]

**SNOOP DOGG** [rapper]: "There [are] certain qualities about Johnny Cash that gangsta rappers like to take and put within themselves, because there's always a good quality about somebody special in the game that you can take something from. Johnny Cash is one of those individuals."[8]

**JACK WHITE** [The White Stripes]: "He's such a man to look up to, just for a male to look up to a man, you know, you can't think of anyone more inspiring than that. People should get down on their knees in front of him for what he's done and the songs he's written."[9]

**TRENT REZNOR** [author of "Hurt," Nine Inch Nails]: "Any exposure to this video or any of Johnny's music may help some people realize the possibilities of music, and [it] reminds you that it doesn't have to all be what it has turned into for the most part."[10]

**SHERYL CROW**: "In a lot of ways, he kind of defined what rock 'n' roll was. You know ... that picture of him flipping off the camera, and he was kind of the radical outlaw, but he was also writing these songs that were just gut wrenching. He's always been who he is, there's never been any question, he's never changed who he was for any kind of popularity. He's always been the Man in Black."[11]

**KID ROCK**: "Johnny Cash's influence on me has been tremendous. It started out when I was a kid with my father's record collection and hearing it around the house with a lot of the other Sun records and whatnot. And then, when I became an age to come full circle from that to hip-hop back to my musical roots, which I was introduced to when I was young, everything that he ever made—[from] his gospel stuff to his outlaw music to anything he ever did. To me, when I see Johnny Cash, I see red, white and black."[12]

**EMMYLOU HARRIS**: "Johnny Cash is the coolest man in the world. I really think they invented the word charisma to describe what Johnny Cash has."[13]

**BONO**: "I would rather spend a day with Johnny Cash than a week with any up-and-coming pop star."[14]

**QUENTIN TARANTINO**: "I've often wondered if gangsta rappers know how little separates their tales of ghetto thug life from Johnny Cash's tales of backwoods thug life. I don't know, but what I do know is Johnny Cash knows ... [but] unlike most gangsta rap, Cash's criminal life songs rarely take place during the high times. In fact, most songs take place after the cell door has slammed shut or a judge's gavel has condemned a man to death."[15]

**KEITH RICHARDS**: "I was a Johnny Cash freak. Luther Perkins, his guitar player, was amazing. Johnny's singing was, too. They taught me about the importance of silence in music—that you don't have to play all over the song. You just play what's necessary. If it's done wrong, it can be painfully monotonous. But when it's done right, it has this incredibly powerful focus and intensity, and that's what those early Cash songs were like. As far as early rock 'n' roll goes, if someone came up to me and for some reason they could only get a collection of one person's music, I'd say, 'Chuck Berry is important, but, man, you've got to get the Cash!'"[16]

**KRIS KRISTOFFERSON**: "I was backstage at the Grand Ole Opry in Nashville when I met him in 1965. It was back in his dangerous days, and it was electric. He was skinny as a snake, and you just never knew what he was going to do. He looked like he might explode at any minute. He was a bad boy, he stood up for the underdog, he was exciting and unpredictable, and he had an energy onstage that was unlike anybody else. I shook hands with him, and that was probably what brought me back to Nashville to be a songwriter. He was everything I thought an artist ought to be."[17]

**RICK RUBIN**: "He's a timeless presence. From the beginning of rock 'n' roll there's always been this dark figure who never really fit. He's still the quintessential outsider. In the hip-hop world you see all these bad boy artists who are juggling being on MTV and running from the law. John was the originator of that."[18]

**A MOM**: "I have a seventeen-year-old son who just hates country-western music, but he's crazy about Johnny Cash. He says Johnny Cash is cool."[19]

**BONO:** "Locusts and honey? Not since John the Baptist has there been a voice like that crying in the wilderness. The most male voice in Christendom. Every man knows he is a sissy compared to Johnny Cash."[20]

# NOTES

INTRODUCTION

## A ONE-MAN MT. RUSHMORE OF AMERICAN ROCK

1. "Johnny on the Spot," *Newsweek* (February 2, 1970): 84.
2. Tom Dearmore, "First Angry Man of Country Singers," *New York Times Magazine* (September 21, 1969): 33.
3. Ibid, 49.
4. "For Cash, the Muse Was Strong Until the End," Associated Press, posted online September 12, 2003.
5. Richard Corliss, "The Man in Black," *Time* (September 22, 2003): 62.
6. Christopher S. Wren, *Winners Got Scars Too: The Life and Legends of Johnny Cash* (New York, N.Y.: The Dial Press, 1971) 149.
7. Johnny Cash, *Man in White* (New York, N.Y.: Harper & Row) 3.
8. Johnny Cash, *Man in Black* (Grand Rapids, Mi.: Zondervan Publishing House, 1975) 32-33.
9. Johnny Cash, *Man in White* (New York, N.Y.: Harper & Row) 16.
10. Johnny Cash with Patrick Carr, *Cash: The Autobiography* (New York, N.Y.: HarperPaperbacks, 1997) 306.
11. George Carpozi, Jr., *The Johnny Cash Story* (New York, N.Y.: Pyramid Books, 1970) 55.
12. Patrick Carr, "Johnny Cash's Freedom" *Country Music* (April 1979): 24-28.
13. Johnny Cash, *Man in Black* (Grand Rapids, Mi.: Zondervan Publishing House, 1975) 33.

14. Ibid, 242.
15. Ibid, 197.
16. Johnny Cash with Patrick Carr, *Cash: The Autobiography* (New York, N.Y.: HarperPaperbacks, 1997) 281.
17. Bill DeYoung, "Johnny Cash: American Music Legend" *Goldmine*, (July 19, 1996).
18. From the liner notes, Cash's *God* album.
19. From the televised *All-Star Tribute to Johnny Cash*, TNT, 1999.
20. Anthony DeCurtis, "Johnny Cash Won't Back Down," *Rolling Stone* (October 26, 2000): 60.
21. Ibid.
22. Johnny Cash with Patrick Carr, *Cash: The Autobiography* (New York, N.Y.: HarperPaperbacks, 1997) 9.
23. From the liner notes, Cash's *Just As I Am* album.
24. Charles Paul Conn, *The New Johnny Cash* (Old Tappan, N.J.: Fleming
H. Revell Company, 1973) 72.
25. Johnny Cash, *Man in Black* (Grand Rapids, Mi.: Zondervan Publishing House, 1975) 21.
26. Wes Orshoski, "Exclusive: Cash's 'American' Outtakes 'Unearthed'" *Billboard*, posted online August 14, 2003.
27. Bill Friskics-Warren, "The Man in Black and White, and Every Shade in Between," *No Depression* (November/December 2002): 82.

## CHAPTER ONE
## I AM BOUND FOR THE PROMISED LAND

1. Tom Dearmore, "First Angry Man of Country Singers," *New York Times Magazine* (September 21, 1969): 39
2. Christopher S. Wren, "The Restless Ballad of Johnny Cash" *Look* (April 29, 1969): 72.
3. Ibid.
4. Tom Dearmore, "First Angry Man of Country Singers," *New York Times Magazine* (September 21, 1969): 37.
5. Christopher S. Wren, *Winners Got Scars Too: The Life and Legends of Johnny Cash* (New York, N.Y.: The Dial Press, 1971) 53.
6. "Cashing In," *Time* (June 6, 1969): 94.
7. Steve Dougherty & Kelly Williams, "Back in Black," *People* (December 23, 2002): 69.
8. Christopher S. Wren, *Winners Got Scars Too: The Life and Legends of Johnny Cash* (New York, N.Y.: The Dial Press, 1971) 43.
9. John Frook, "Hard-Times King of Song," *Life* (November 21, 1969): 48.
10. "Cashing In," *Time* (June 6, 1969): 94.
11. Johnny Cash, *Man in Black* (Grand Rapids, Mi.: Zondervan Publishing House, 1975) 23.
12. Christopher S. Wren, *Winners Got Scars Too: The Life and Legends of Johnny Cash* (New York, N.Y.: The Dial Press, 1971) 23.

13. George Carpozi, Jr., *The Johnny Cash Story* (New York, N.Y.: Pyramid Books, 1970) 29.
14. Charles Paul Conn, *The New Johnny Cash* (Old Tappan, N.J.: Fleming H. Revell Company, 1973) 30-31.
15. Johnny Cash, *Man in Black* (Grand Rapids, Mi.: Zondervan Publishing House, 1975) 24-25.
16. Ibid, 25.
17. Ibid, 26-27.
18. Ibid, 37-38.
19. Ibid.
20. Ibid, 38.
21. Johnny Cash with Patrick Carr, *Cash: The Autobiography* (New York, N.Y.: HarperPaperbacks, 1997) 321.
22. Christopher S. Wren, *Winners Got Scars Too: The Life and Legends of Johnny Cash* (New York, N.Y.: The Dial Press, 1971) 55.
23. Johnny Cash with Patrick Carr, *Cash: The Autobiography* (New York, N.Y.: HarperPaperbacks, 1997) 321.
24. Johnny Cash with Patrick Carr, *Cash: The Autobiography* (New York, N.Y.: HarperPaperbacks, 1997) 319.
25. Christopher S. Wren, *Winners Got Scars Too: The Life and Legends of Johnny Cash* (New York, N.Y.: The Dial Press, 1971) 55.
26. Christopher S. Wren, *Winners Got Scars Too: The Life and Legends of Johnny Cash* (New York, N.Y.: The Dial Press, 1971) 48.

## CHAPTER TWO
## CAN YOU HEAR THE ANGELS?

1. Johnny Cash, *Man in White* (New York, N.Y.: Harper & Row) 13.
2. Johnny Cash with Patrick Carr, *Cash: The Autobiography* (New York, N.Y.: HarperPaperbacks, 1997) 30.
3. Johnny Cash, *Man in Black* (Grand Rapids, Mi.: Zondervan Publishing House, 1975) 32.
4. Johnny Cash with Patrick Carr, *Cash: The Autobiography* (New York, N.Y.: HarperPaperbacks, 1997) 31.
5. Ibid.
6. Ibid.
7. Ibid, 32.
8. Ibid, 32-33.
9. Ibid, 33.
10. Ibid, 34.
11. Ibid, 35-36.
12. June Carter Cash, *From the Heart* (New York, N.Y.: Prentice Hall Press, a division of Simon & Schuster, Inc., 1987) 26.
13. Johnny Cash with Patrick Carr, *Cash: The Autobiography* (New York, N.Y.: HarperPaperbacks, 1997) 36-37.
14. Ibid.
15. Nick Tosches, "Chordless in Gaza: The Second Coming of John R.

Cash," *The Journal of Country Music* (17, no. 3, 1995).

16. Johnny Cash with Patrick Carr, *Cash: The Autobiography* (New York, N.Y.: HarperPaperbacks, 1997) 321.
17. Ibid.
18. Charles Paul Conn, *The New Johnny Cash* (Old Tappan, N.J.: Fleming H. Revell Company, 1973) 32.
19. Johnny Cash with Patrick Carr, *Cash: The Autobiography* (New York, N.Y.: HarperPaperbacks, 1997) 38.
20. Ibid, 39.
21. Ibid.

## CHAPTER THREE
## GOD'S GOT HIS HAND ON YOU

1. Steve Dougherty & Kelly Williams, "Back in Black," *People* (December 23, 2002): 69.
2. George Carpozi, Jr., *The Johnny Cash Story* (New York, N.Y.: Pyramid Books, 1970) 29.
3. John Frook, "Hard-Times King of Song," *Life* (November 21, 1969): 48.
4. Johnny Cash with Patrick Carr, *Cash: The Autobiography* (New York, N.Y.: HarperPaperbacks, 1997) 66.
5. Ibid, 69.
6. Christopher S. Wren, *Winners Got Scars Too: The Life and Legends of Johnny Cash* (New York, N.Y.: The Dial Press, 1971) 66.
7. Johnny Cash with Patrick Carr, *Cash: The Autobiography* (New York, N.Y.: HarperPaperbacks, 1997) 71.
8. Christopher S. Wren, *Winners Got Scars Too: The Life and Legends of Johnny Cash* (New York, N.Y.: The Dial Press, 1971) 57.
9. Johnny Cash with Patrick Carr, *Cash: The Autobiography* (New York, N.Y.: HarperPaperbacks, 1997) 70-71.
10. Ibid, 69.
11. Ibid, 71.
12. Ibid, 72.
13. John Frook, "Hard-Times King of Song," *Life* (November 21, 1969): 48.
14. Johnny Cash with Patrick Carr, *Cash: The Autobiography* (New York, N.Y.: HarperPaperbacks, 1997) 72-73.
15. Charles Paul Conn, *The New Johnny Cash* (Old Tappan, N.J.: Fleming H. Revell Company, 1973) 31.
16. Christopher S. Wren, *Winners Got Scars Too: The Life and Legends of Johnny Cash* (New York, N.Y.: The Dial Press, 1971) 65.

## CHAPTER FOUR
## WANDERLUST WHETTED

1. Christopher S. Wren, *Winners Got Scars Too: The Life and Legends of Johnny Cash* (New York, N.Y.: The Dial Press, 1971) 67-69.
2. Johnny Cash with Patrick Carr, *Cash: The Autobiography* (New York,

N.Y.: HarperPaperbacks, 1997) 83.
3. Johnny Cash, *Man in Black* (Grand Rapids, Mi.: Zondervan Publishing House, 1975) 67.
4. Christopher S. Wren, *Winners Got Scars Too: The Life and Legends of Johnny Cash* (New York, N.Y.: The Dial Press, 1971) 71.
5. Ibid, 72-73.
6. Steve Dougherty & Kelly Williams, "Back in Black," *People* (December 23, 2002): 69.
7. "Music Legend Fades to Black," Associated Press, posted on the Internet, September 12, 2003.
8. Johnny Cash with Patrick Carr, *Cash: The Autobiography* (New York, N.Y.: HarperPaperbacks, 1997) 82.
9. Ibid, 195.
10. Johnny Cash, *Man in Black* (Grand Rapids, Mi.: Zondervan Publishing House, 1975) 69.
11. Ibid, 95.
12. Christopher S. Wren, *Winners Got Scars Too: The Life and Legends of Johnny Cash* (New York, N.Y.: The Dial Press, 1971) 76.
13. Ibid, 78.
14. Ibid, 80.
15. Johnny Cash with Patrick Carr, *Cash: The Autobiography* (New York, N.Y.: HarperPaperbacks, 1997) 94.
16. Christopher S. Wren, *Winners Got Scars Too: The Life and Legends of Johnny Cash* (New York, N.Y.: The Dial Press, 1971) 82.
17. Ibid, 89.
18. Johnny Cash with Patrick Carr, *Cash: The Autobiography* (New York, N.Y.: HarperPaperbacks, 1997) 98-99.
19. By John R. Cash, copyright 1964, Southwind Music, Inc.
20. Johnny Cash with Patrick Carr, *Cash: The Autobiography* (New York, N.Y.: HarperPaperbacks, 1997) 86.
21. Christopher S. Wren, *Winners Got Scars Too: The Life and Legends of Johnny Cash* (New York, N.Y.: The Dial Press, 1971) 83.

## CHAPTER FIVE
## COME ON IN!

1. Steve Dougherty & Kelly Williams, "Back in Black," *People* (December 23, 2002): 69.
2. Johnny Cash with Patrick Carr, *Cash: The Autobiography* (New York, N.Y.: HarperPaperbacks, 1997) 113.
3. Ibid, 100.
4. Hank Davis, "Johnny Cash: The Sun Sound," *Goldmine* (December 20, 1985).
5. Christopher S. Wren, *Winners Got Scars Too: The Life and Legends of Johnny Cash* (New York, N.Y.: The Dial Press, 1971) 88.
6. Johnny Cash with Patrick Carr, *Cash: The Autobiography* (New York, N.Y.: HarperPaperbacks, 1997) 65.

7. Ibid, 166-167.
8. Christopher S. Wren, *Winners Got Scars Too: The Life and Legends of Johnny Cash* (New York, N.Y.: The Dial Press, 1971) 90.
9. Johnny Cash with Patrick Carr, *Cash: The Autobiography* (New York, N.Y.: HarperPaperbacks, 1997) 196.
10. Johnny Cash, *Man in Black* (Grand Rapids, Mi.: Zondervan Publishing House, 1975) 78.
11. Johnny Cash with Patrick Carr, *Cash: The Autobiography* (New York, N.Y.: HarperPaperbacks, 1997) 122-123.
12. Bill Friskics-Warren, "The Man in Black and White, and Every Shade in Between," *No Depression* (November/December 2002): 90.
13. Johnny Cash with Patrick Carr, *Cash: The Autobiography* (New York, N.Y.: HarperPaperbacks, 1997) 122-123.
14. Johnny Cash with Patrick Carr, *Cash: The Autobiography* (New York, N.Y.: HarperPaperbacks, 1997) 130.
15. "The Jukebox" *Time* (February 23, 1959): 66.
16. Christopher S. Wren, *Winners Got Scars Too: The Life and Legends of Johnny Cash* (New York, N.Y.: The Dial Press, 1971) 105.

## CHAPTER SIX
## DEMON PILL POSSESSION

1. "Penthouse Interview: Johnny Cash," by Larry Linderman, *Penthouse*, August 1975, as reprinted in *Ring of Fire: The Johnny Cash Reader*, Michael Streissguth (ed.) (Cambridge, MA: Da Capo Press, Perseus Books Group, 2002) 152.
2. Johnny Cash with Patrick Carr, *Cash: The Autobiography* (New York, N.Y.: HarperPaperbacks, 1997) 191.
3. Ibid, 192.
4. Ibid, 193.
5. Ibid, 190-191.
6. Ibid, 196-197.
7. Ibid, 201.
8. "Penthouse Interview: Johnny Cash," by Larry Linderman, *Penthouse*, August 1975, as reprinted in *Ring of Fire: The Johnny Cash Reader*, Michael Streissguth (ed.) (Cambridge, MA: Da Capo Press, Perseus Books Group, 2002) 150.
9. Johnny Cash with Patrick Carr, *Cash: The Autobiography* (New York, N.Y.: HarperPaperbacks, 1997) 268-269.
10. By June Carter/Merle Kilgore in 193 from *Ring of Fire* (Columbia CS 8853)
11. Steve Dougherty & Kelly Williams, "Back in Black," *People* (December 23, 2002): 69.
12. Anthony DeCurtis, "Johnny Cash Won't Back Down," *Rolling Stone* (October 26, 2000): 60.
13. Ibid.
14. Ibid.

15. Johnny Cash with Patrick Carr, *Cash: The Autobiography* (New York, N.Y.: HarperPaperbacks, 1997) 202.
16. Ibid, 203, 206.
17. Christopher S. Wren, *Winners Got Scars Too: The Life and Legends of Johnny Cash* (New York, N.Y.: The Dial Press, 1971) 152.
18. By Peter LaFarge, arr. Bob Dylan, copyright 1962, 1964, Edward B. Marks Music Company.
19. Johnny Cash with Patrick Carr, *Cash: The Autobiography* (New York, N.Y.: HarperPaperbacks, 1997) 223.
20. Ibid, 225.
21. Ibid, 229.
22. Johnny Cash, *Man in Black* (Grand Rapids, Mi.: Zondervan Publishing House, 1975) 19.
23. Ibid, 110.
24. Ibid, 109.
25. Ibid, 113.
26. Charles Paul Conn, *The New Johnny Cash* (Old Tappan, N.J.: Fleming H. Revell Company, 1973) 22.
27. Johnny Cash, *Man in Black* (Grand Rapids, Mi.: Zondervan Publishing House, 1975) 137.
28. Richard Corliss, "The Man in Black," *Time* (September 22, 2003): 64.
29. Christopher S. Wren, *Winners Got Scars Too: The Life and Legends of Johnny Cash* (New York, N.Y.: The Dial Press, 1971) 175-176.
30. Ibid, 159-160.
31. Charles Paul Conn, *The New Johnny Cash* (Old Tappan, N.J.: Fleming H. Revell Company, 1973) 23-24.
32. Christopher S. Wren, *Winners Got Scars Too: The Life and Legends of Johnny Cash* (New York, N.Y.: The Dial Press, 1971) 186.
33. Johnny Cash, *Man in Black* (Grand Rapids, Mi.: Zondervan Publishing House, 1975) 20.

## CHAPTER SEVEN
## NICKAJACK CAVE & THE WAY HOME

1. Johnny Cash with Patrick Carr, *Cash: The Autobiography* (New York, N.Y.: HarperPaperbacks, 1997) 230.
2. Nick Tosches, "Chordless in Gaza: The Second Coming of John R. Cash," *The Journal of Country Music* (17, no. 3, 1995).
3. Ibid.
4. Johnny Cash with Patrick Carr, *Cash: The Autobiography* (New York, N.Y.: HarperPaperbacks, 1997) 231.
5. Ibid.
6. Ibid, 231-232.
7. Nick Tosches, "Chordless in Gaza: The Second Coming of John R. Cash," *The Journal of Country Music* (17, no. 3, 1995).
8. Johnny Cash with Patrick Carr, *Cash: The Autobiography* (New York, N.Y.: HarperPaperbacks, 1997) 232.

9. Ibid, 233.
10. Charles Paul Conn, *The New Johnny Cash* (Old Tappan, N.J.: Fleming H. Revell Company, 1973) 26.
11. Anthony DeCurtis, "Johnny Cash Won't Back Down," *Rolling Stone* (October 26, 2000): 60.
12. Johnny Cash, *Man in Black* (Grand Rapids, Mi.: Zondervan Publishing House, 1975) 144.
13. Ibid, 145.
14. Christopher S. Wren, *Winners Got Scars Too: The Life and Legends of Johnny Cash* (New York, N.Y.: The Dial Press, 1971) 190.
15. Ibid, 194.
16. Christopher S. Wren, *Winners Got Scars Too: The Life and Legends of Johnny Cash* (New York, N.Y.: The Dial Press, 1971) 195.
17. Johnny Cash, *Man in Black* (Grand Rapids, Mi.: Zondervan Publishing House, 1975) 161.
18. Johnny Cash with Patrick Carr, *Cash: The Autobiography* (New York, N.Y.: HarperPaperbacks, 1997) 235.
19. Richard Corliss, "The Man in Black," *Time* (September 22, 2003): 64.
20. Johnny Cash, *Man in Black* (Grand Rapids, Mi.: Zondervan Publishing House, 1975) 149.

## CHAPTER EIGHT
## BEHOLD, ALL THINGS BECOME NEW

1. Johnny Cash with Patrick Carr, *Cash: The Autobiography* (New York, N.Y.: HarperPaperbacks, 1997) 253.
2. Johnny Cash, *Man in Black* (Grand Rapids, Mi.: Zondervan Publishing House, 1975) 22.
3. Johnny Cash with Patrick Carr, *Cash: The Autobiography* (New York, N.Y.: HarperPaperbacks, 1997) 305.
4. Johnny Cash, *Man in White* (New York, N.Y.: Harper & Row) 5.
5. Johnny Cash with Patrick Carr, *Cash: The Autobiography* (New York, N.Y.: HarperPaperbacks, 1997) 305.
6. Ibid.
7. Ibid, 269.
8. Ibid, 270.
9. Tom Dearmore, "First Angry Man of Country Singers," *New York Times Magazine* (September 21, 1969): 54.
10. "Johnny on the Spot," *Newsweek*, (February 2, 1970): 84.
11. "Penthouse Interview: Johnny Cash," by Larry Linderman, *Penthouse*, August 1975, as reprinted in *Ring of Fire: The Johnny Cash Reader*, Michael Streissguth (ed.) (Cambridge, MA: Da Capo Press, Perseus Books Group, 2002) 157.
12. Johnny Cash, *Man in Black* (Grand Rapids, Mi.: Zondervan Publishing House, 1975) 153.
13. Alfred G. Arnowitz, "Music Behind the Bars" *Life* (August 16, 1968): 12.
14. "Empathy in the Dungeon" *Time* (August 30, 1968): 52.

15. From a CMT network special, "Inside Fame"
16. Lyrics by Shel Silverstein, copyright 1969 Sony Music
17. Bill Flanagan, "Johnny Cash, American" *Musician* (May 1988).
18. Johnny Cash, *Man in Black* (Grand Rapids, Mi.: Zondervan Publishing House, 1975) 164.
19. Richard Corliss, "The Man in Black," *Time* (September 22, 2003): 64.
20. Johnny Cash with Patrick Carr, *Cash: The Autobiography* (New York, N.Y.: HarperPaperbacks, 1997) 314.
21. Steve Dougherty & Kelly Williams, "Back in Black," *People* (December 23, 2002): 69.
22. Anthony DeCurtis, "Johnny Cash Won't Back Down," *Rolling Stone* (October 26, 2000): 60.

## CHAPTER NINE
## THE JOHNNY CASH SHOW

1. Bill Friskics-Warren, "The Man in Black and White, and Every Shade in Between," *No Depression* (November/December 2002): 86.
2. Johnny Cash with Patrick Carr, *Cash: The Autobiography* (New York, N.Y.: HarperPaperbacks, 1997) 266.
3. Tom Dearmore, "First Angry Man of Country Singers," *New York Times Magazine* (September 21, 1969): 42.
4. Johnny Cash, *Man in Black* (Grand Rapids, Mi.: Zondervan Publishing House, 1975) 197.
5. Words and music by Arthur Smith, copyright 1954, Lynn Music Company.
6. Johnny Cash with Patrick Carr, *Cash: The Autobiography* (New York, N.Y.: HarperPaperbacks, 1997) 275.
7. Ibid, 278.
8. Johnny Cash, *Man in Black* (Grand Rapids, Mi.: Zondervan Publishing House, 1975) 201.
9. Tom Dearmore, "First Angry Man of Country Singers," *New York Times Magazine* (September 21, 1969): 34.
10. Ibid, 42.
11. Ibid, 35.
12. Robert Shelton, "Johnny Cash Sings to a Full House: Presents Country Soul in Comeback at Carnegie" *New York Times* (October 24, 1968): 51.
13. Richard Goldstein, "Johnny Cash, 'Something Rude Showing'" *Vogue* (August 15, 1969).

## CHAPTER TEN
## ALTAR CALL

1. Charles Paul Conn, *The New Johnny Cash* (Old Tappan, N.J.: Fleming H. Revell Company, 1973) 36.
2. Ibid, 36-37.
3. Ibid, 37.

4. Ibid, 35.
5. From a CMT network interview.
6. Johnny Cash, *Man in Black* (Grand Rapids, Mi.: Zondervan Publishing House, 1975) 203.
7. Charles Paul Conn, *The New Johnny Cash* (Old Tappan, N.J.: Fleming H. Revell Company, 1973) 39.
8. Johnny Cash, *Man in Black* (Grand Rapids, Mi.: Zondervan Publishing House, 1975) 208.
9. Charles Paul Conn, *The New Johnny Cash* (Old Tappan, N.J.: Fleming H. Revell Company, 1973) 40.
10. Ibid, 39-40.
11. Ibid, 69.
12. Ibid, 67.
13. Ibid, 68-69.
14. Johnny Cash with Patrick Carr, *Cash: The Autobiography* (New York, N.Y.: HarperPaperbacks, 1997) 281.
15. Peter McCabe and Jack Killion, "Interview with Johnny Cash" *Country Music* (May 1973): 24-31.
16. By John R. Cash, copyright 1970 by House of Cash, Inc.
17. Johnny Cash with Patrick Carr, *Cash: The Autobiography* (New York, N.Y.: HarperPaperbacks, 1997) 283.
18. Charles Paul Conn, *The New Johnny Cash* (Old Tappan, N.J.: Fleming H. Revell Company, 1973) 72-73.
19. Ibid, 73-74.
20. Johnny Cash with Patrick Carr, *Cash: The Autobiography* (New York, N.Y.: HarperPaperbacks, 1997) 300.
21. Charles Paul Conn, *The New Johnny Cash* (Old Tappan, N.J.: Fleming H. Revell Company, 1973) 75.
22. Ibid, 78.
23. Ibid, 77.
24. Ibid, 72.
25. Johnny Cash with Patrick Carr, *Cash: The Autobiography* (New York, N.Y.: HarperPaperbacks, 1997) 279.
26. Dorothy Gallagher, "Johnny Cash: 'I'm Growing, I'm Changing, I'm Becoming'," *Redbook* (August 1971).
27. Charles Paul Conn, *The New Johnny Cash* (Old Tappan, N.J.: Fleming H. Revell Company, 1973) 9-10.

## CHAPTER ELEVEN
## GOSPEL ROAD

1. Kenneth L. Woodward, "A Country Jesus," *Newsweek* (January 29, 1973): 50.
2. Johnny Cash with Patrick Carr, *Cash: The Autobiography* (New York, N.Y.: HarperPaperbacks, 1997) 308.
3. Ibid.
4. Charles Paul Conn, *The New Johnny Cash* (Old Tappan, N.J.: Fleming H.

Revell Company, 1973) 83.
5. Ibid.
6. Ibid, 81.
7. George Vecsey, "Cash's 'Gospel Road' Film Is Renaissance for Him," *New York Times* (December 13, 1973): 62.
8. Charles Paul Conn, *The New Johnny Cash* (Old Tappan, N.J.: Fleming H. Revell Company, 1973) 86.
9. Peter McCabe and Jack Killion, "Interview with Johnny Cash" *Country Music* (May 1973): 24-31.
10. Charles Paul Conn, *The New Johnny Cash* (Old Tappan, N.J.: Fleming H. Revell Company, 1973) 82.
11. Johnny Cash, *Man in Black* (Grand Rapids, Mi.: Zondervan Publishing House, 1975) 216.
12. Kenneth L. Woodward, "A Country Jesus," *Newsweek* (January 29, 1973): 50.
13. Johnny Cash with Patrick Carr, *Cash: The Autobiography* (New York, N.Y.: HarperPaperbacks, 1997) 309-310.
14. Ibid, 310-311.
15. Charles Paul Conn, *The New Johnny Cash* (Old Tappan, N.J.: Fleming H. Revell Company, 1973) 83.
16. From the liner notes of *Kris Kristofferson: Singer/Songwriter*, copyright 1991 Sony Music.
17. Johnny Cash, *Man in Black* (Grand Rapids, Mi.: Zondervan Publishing House, 1975) 220.
18. Ibid, 222.
19. Ibid.
20. Billy Graham, *Just As I Am: The Autobiography of Billy Graham* (HarperCollins/Bondservant, 1997): 437.
21. Kenneth L. Woodward, "A Country Jesus," *Newsweek* (January 29, 1973): 50.

## CHAPTER TWELVE
## MEETING THE MAN IN WHITE

1. Joyce Maynard, "Cash Sings Gospel of Old Values," *New York Times* (November 19, 1976): C28.
2. Michael Streissguth (ed.), *Ring of Fire: The Johnny Cash Reader* (Cambridge, MA: Da Capo Press, Perseus Books Group, 2002) xviii
3. Ibid, xix.
4. Steve Pond, "Johnny Cash: The Hard Reign of a Country Music King," *Rolling Stone* (December 10 & 24, 1992): 118.
5. Johnny Cash with Patrick Carr, *Cash: The Autobiography* (New York, N.Y.: HarperPaperbacks, 1997) 329.
6. Ibid, 240.
7. Ibid, 240-241.
8. Johnny Cash, *Man in White* (New York, N.Y.: Harper & Row) 11.
9. Johnny Cash with Patrick Carr, *Cash: The Autobiography* (New York,

N.Y.: HarperPaperbacks, 1997) 243, 246.
10. Ibid, 247.
11. Ibid, 248.
12 Ibid, 311.
13 Johnny Cash, *Man in White* (New York, N.Y.: Harper & Row) 9.
14. Johnny Cash with Patrick Carr, *Cash: The Autobiography* (New York, N.Y.: HarperPaperbacks, 1997) 319.
15. Johnny Cash, *Man in White* (New York, N.Y.: Harper & Row) 14-15.
16. Johnny Cash with Patrick Carr, *Cash: The Autobiography* (New York, N.Y.: HarperPaperbacks, 1997) 312.
17. Neil Strauss, "New Rebel for the 90's: Meet Johnny Cash, 62" *New York Times* (September 14, 1994) C18.
18. Johnny Cash with Patrick Carr, *Cash: The Autobiography* (New York, N.Y.: HarperPaperbacks, 1997) 353.
19. Neil Strauss, "New Rebel for the 90's: Meet Johnny Cash, 62" *New York Times* (September 14, 1994) C18.

## CHAPTER THIRTEEN
## THE WANDERER

1. Greg Kot, "Johnny Cash: New Godfather of Cool," *Chicago Tribune* (December 8, 1996).
2. Steve Pond, "Johnny Cash: The Hard Reign of a Country Music King," *Rolling Stone* (December 10 & 24, 1992): 118.
3. Jancee Dunn, "Johnny Cash," *Rolling Stone* (June 30, 1994): 35
4. Niall Stokes, *Into the Heart: The Stories Behind Every U2 Song* (New York, N.Y.: Thunder's Mouth Press, 1996) 122.
5. By U2, copyright 1993 by PolyGram International Music.
6. Niall Stokes, *Into the Heart: The Stories Behind Every U2 Song* (New York, N.Y.: Thunder's Mouth Press, 1996) 123.
7. Ibid.
8. Bill Flanagan, *U2 at the End of the World* (Dell Publishing, a division of Bantam Doubleday Dell Publishing Group, Inc., 1995) 224.
9. Niall Stokes, *Into the Heart: The Stories Behind Every U2 Song* (New York, N.Y.: Thunder's Mouth Press, 1996) 123.
10. Ibid.

## CHAPTER FOURTEEN
## AMERICAN RECORDINGS

1. Steve Pond, "Johnny Cash: The Hard Reign of a Country Music King," *Rolling Stone* (December 10 & 24, 1992): 118.
2. Johnny Cash with Patrick Carr, *Cash: The Autobiography* (New York, N.Y.: HarperPaperbacks, 1997) 345.
3. Bill Shaw, "Easing Back with ... Johnny Cash," *People*, (July 11, 1994): 100.
4. Greg Kot, "Johnny Cash: New Godfather of Cool," *Chicago Tribune*

(December 8, 1996).
5. Wes Orshoski, "Johnny Cash: An American Original," *Billboard* (March 30, 2002): 1.
6. Jancee Dunn, "Johnny Cash," *Rolling Stone* (June 30, 1994): 35
7. Greg Kot, "Johnny Cash: New Godfather of Cool," *Chicago Tribune* (December 8, 1996).
8. Lyrics by Johnny Cash/ Music by D. Troops and K. Sibersdorf.
9. Greg Kot, "Johnny Cash: New Godfather of Cool," *Chicago Tribune* (December 8, 1996).
10. Renee Graham, "Life in the Pop Lane: With MTV Nomination, Another Generation Discovers Cash's Cool," *Boston Globe* (July 29, 2003): E1
11. Greg Kot, "Johnny Cash: New Godfather of Cool," *Chicago Tribune* (December 8, 1996).
12. By Johnny Cash, copyright 1994, published by Song of Cash, Inc.
13. Jancee Dunn, "Johnny Cash," *Rolling Stone* (June 30, 1994): 35
14. Neil Strauss, "New Rebel for the 90's: Meet Johnny Cash, 62" *New York Times* (September 14, 1994) C18.
15. Johnny Cash with Patrick Carr, *Cash: The Autobiography* (New York, N.Y.: HarperPaperbacks, 1997) 347.
16. Jancee Dunn, "Johnny Cash," *Rolling Stone* (June 30, 1994): 35
17. From a CMT televised interview.
18. Johnny Cash with Patrick Carr, *Cash: The Autobiography* (New York, N.Y.: HarperPaperbacks, 1997) 347.

## CHAPTER FIFTEEN
## UNCHAINED

1. Paul Verna, "Johnny Cash Courts Young Fans," *Billboard* (October 12, 1996): 18.
2. By Chris Cornell, copyright 1991, published by You Make Me Sick I Make Music (ASCAP).
3. From MTV.com.
4. Greg Kot, "Johnny Cash: New Godfather of Cool," *Chicago Tribune* (December 8, 1996).
5. Paul Verna, "Johnny Cash Courts Young Fans," *Billboard* (October 12, 1996): 18.
6. Greg Kot, "Johnny Cash: New Godfather of Cool," *Chicago Tribune* (December 8, 1996)
7. Paul Verna, "Johnny Cash Courts Young Fans," *Billboard* (October 12, 1996): 18.
8. Greg Kot, "Johnny Cash: New Godfather of Cool," *Chicago Tribune* (December 8, 1996).
9. From the liner notes of Johnny Cash's *Unchained* album, copyright 1996 *American Recordings*.
10. John R. Cash, copyright 1996, published by Songs of Cash, Inc. (ASCAP), administered by BUG music.
11. From the *Unchained* bio.

12. By Josh Haden, published by Angel Heutebise (BMI).
13. Greg Kot, "Johnny Cash: New Godfather of Cool," *Chicago Tribune* (December 8, 1996).
14. Chuck Taylor & Deborah Evans Price, "Cash Ad Stirs It Up," *Billboard* (April 11, 1998).
15. Ibid.
16. Ibid.

## CHAPTER SIXTEEN
## SOLITARY MAN

1. Peter Cooper and Craig Havighurst, "Country Music Legend Johnny Cash Dead at 71," *The Tennessean* (September 12, 2003), retrieved September 17, 2003 from www.tennessean.com/entertainment/news/archives/03/09/39209092.shtml
2. Anthony DeCurtis, "Johnny Cash Won't Back Down," *Rolling Stone* (October 26, 2000): 60.
3. Jason Fine, "A Day in the Life of Johnny Cash," *Rolling Stone* (December 12, 2002): 46.
4. Luke Torn, "Still Keeping His Eyes Wide Open," *Wall Street Journal* (November 15, 2002): W11.
5. Brian Mansfield, "Reserved Johnny Cash: He Won't Back Down," CDNOW.com web profiles (January 2001).
6. Wes Orshoski, "Johnny Cash: An American Original," *Billboard* (March 30, 2002): 1.
7. Brian Mansfield, "Reserved Johnny Cash: He Won't Back Down," CDNOW.com web profiles (January 2001).
8. By Tom Petty & Jeff Lynne.
9. By Haven Gillespie & Beasley Smith, copyright 1949, Renewed 1977 Robbins Music Corp.
10. By Nick Cave & Mick Harvey.
11. Brian Mansfield, "Reserved Johnny Cash: He Won't Back Down," CDNOW.com web profiles (January 2001).
12. From the *Solitary Man* liner notes.
13. From http://www.dylanchords.com/00_misc/mary_of_the_wild_moor.htm, accessed September 18, 2003.
14. From the *Solitary Man* liner notes.

## CHAPTER SEVENTEEN
## THE MAN COMES AROUND

1. Steve Dougherty & Kelly Williams, "Back in Black," *People* (December 23, 2002): 69.
2. Eric R. Danton, "Johnny Cash, the Man in Black: An American Legend," *Hartford Courant,* (November 3, 2002): G1.
3. Ibid.
4. Richard Corliss, "The Man in Black," *Time* (September 22, 2003): 60.

5. Richard Harrington, "Despite Age and Illness, a Steady Cash Flow," *Washington Post* (November 3, 2002): G1.
6. Steve Dougherty & Kelly Williams, "Back in Black," *People* (December 23, 2002): 69.
7. Eric R. Danton, "Johnny Cash, the Man in Black: An American Legend," *Hartford Courant*, (November 3, 2002): G1.
8. Ben Wener, "Johnny, Paul: In Sickness and in Health," *Orange County Register* (November 1, 2002): Music1.
9. Jim Farber, "Cash Reward: In the Rush to Memorialize Johnny, the Man Himself Beats All Comers," *New York Daily News* (November 3, 2002): 19.
10. Ibid.
11. By John R. Cash, copyright 2002, Song of Cash Music, Inc. (ASCAP).
12. Luke Torn, "Still Keeping His Eyes Wide Open," *Wall Street Journal* (November 15, 2002): W11.
13. Andrew Dansby, "Springsteen, Dylan Get Rhythm," *Rolling Stone* (February 21, 2002).
14. Joe D'Angelo, "Johnny Cash Says Unlike Most Videos, 'Hurt' Wasn't Too Painful" MTV.com (August 26, 2003).
15. Eric R. Danton, "Johnny Cash, the Man in Black: An American Legend," *Hartford Courant*, (November 3, 2002): G1.
16. Jim Farber, "Cash Reward: In the Rush to Memorialize Johnny, the Man Himself Beats All Comers," *New York Daily News* (November 3, 2002): 19.
17. Luke Torn, "Still Keeping His Eyes Wide Open," *Wall Street Journal* (November 15, 2002): W11.
18. Ben Wener, "Johnny, Paul: In Sickness and in Health," *Orange County Register* (November 1, 2002): Music1.
19. Robert Hilburn, "At Home and at Peace," *Los Angeles Times* (October 20, 2002): E42.
20. Jim Farber, "Cash Reward: In the Rush to Memorialize Johnny, the Man Himself Beats All Comers," *New York Daily News* (November 3, 2002): 19.

## CHAPTER EIGHTEEN
## HURT

1. "Johnny Cash's 'Hurt' Delves into Life of Former Hell-Raiser: VMA Lens Recap," MTV.com, (February 27, 2003).
2. Mark Binelli, "Video of the Year! Johnny Cash's 'Hurt' Leaves Viewers Speechless," *Rolling Stone* (March 6, 2003): 28.
3. Ibid.
4. "Johnny Cash's 'Hurt' Delves into Life of Former Hell-Raiser: VMA Lens Recap," MTV.com, (February 27, 2003).
5. Ibid.
6. Brian Mansfield, *USA Today* (January 31, 2003).
7. Geoff Boucher, "Who's That Between Audioslave, Beck?" *Los Angeles*

*Times* (February 17, 2003): E3.
8. David Bauder, "Johnny Cash May Steal Show at MTV Awards," Associated Press (August 24, 2003).
9. Geoff Boucher, "Who's That Between Audioslave, Beck?" *Los Angeles Times* (February 17, 2003): E3.
10. Mark Binelli, "Video of the Year! Johnny Cash's 'Hurt' Leaves Viewers Speechless," *Rolling Stone* (March 6, 2003): 28.
11. David Bauder, "Johnny Cash May Steal Show at MTV Awards," AP (August 24, 2003).
12. Ibid.
13. Eric R. Danton, "Johnny Cash, the Man in Black: An American Legend," *Hartford Courant*, (November 3, 2002): G1.
14. "Johnny Cash's 'Hurt' Delves into Life of Former Hell-Raiser: VMA Lens Recap," MTV.com, (February 27, 2003).
15. David Bauder, "Johnny Cash May Steal Show at MTV Awards," Associated Press (August 24, 2003).
16. Joe D'Angelo, "Johnny Cash Says Unlike Most Videos, 'Hurt' Wasn't Too Painful" MTV.com (August 26, 2003).
17. Richard Corliss, "The Man in Black," *Time* (September 22, 2003): 62.

## CHAPTER NINETEEN
## EVERYONE I KNOW GOES AWAY IN THE END

1. From *USAToday.com*, posted February 14, 2002.
2. From *CNN.com*, posted February 26, 2003.
3. Joal Ryan, *www.eonline.com*, posted July 31, 2003.
4. Kurt Loder, "Johnny Cash: Original Gangsta," *MTV.com*.
5. From *www.JohnnyCash.com*, accessed September 19, 2003.
6. *Time*, August 14, 2003.
7. Erin Curry, "Though Drugs & Alcohol Had Plagued Him, Johnny Cash Was Steadied by His Faith," *BP* (September 12, 2003).
8. Richard Corliss, "The Man in Black," *Time* (September 22, 2003): 66.
9. Ibid.
10. Kurt Loder, "Johnny Cash: Original Gangsta," MTV.com.
11. Johnny Cash with Patrick Carr, *Cash: The Autobiography* (New York, N.Y.: HarperPaperbacks, 1997) 402.
12. Richard Corliss, "The Man in Black," *Time* (September 22, 2003): 66.

## TRIBUTES

1. Billy Graham, *Just As I Am: The Autobiography of Billy Graham* (HarperCollins/Zondervan, 1997) 687, 688.
2. From *VH1.com*.
3. Ibid.
4. Ibid.
5. Ibid.
6. Ibid.

7. Ibid.
8. Ibid.
9. Ibid.
10. Ibid.
11. Ibid.
12. Ibid.
13. Steve Pond, "Johnny Cash: The Hard Reign of a Country Music King," *Rolling Stone* (December 10 & 24, 1992): 118.
14. Ibid.
15. By Quentin Tarantino, from the liner notes to the *Murder* CD.
16. Anthony DeCurtis, "Johnny Cash Won't Back Down," *Rolling Stone* (October 26, 2000): 60.
17. Ibid.
18. Ibid.
19. Tom Dearmore, "First Angry Man of Country Singers," *New York Times Magazine* (September 21, 1969): 34.
20. From the liner notes of *The Essential Johnny Cash*.